Handbook of Measurements for Marriage and Family Therapy

Handbook of Measurements for Marriage and Family Therapy

by Norman Fredman, Ph.D.

&

Robert Sherman, Ed.D.

Queens College, New York

Routledge
Taylor & Francis Group
LONDON AND NEW YORK

First published 1987 by
BRUNNER/MAZEL, INC.

Published 2014 by Routledge
2 Park Square, Milton Park, Abingdon, Oxfordshire OX14 4RN
711 Third Avenue, New York, NY 10017

Routledge is an imprint of the Taylor & Francis Group, an informa business

First issued in paperback 2014

Library of Congress Cataloging-in-Publication Data

Fredman, Norman, 1932-
Handbook of measurements for marriage and family therapy.

Includes bibliographies.
1. Family psychotherapy. 2. Marital psychotherapy.
3. Psychological tests. 4. Psychotherapy patients—Psychological testing. I. Sherman, Robert, 1928-
II. Title. [DNLM: 1. Family Therapy—handbooks.
2. Marital Therapy—handbooks, 3. Psychological Tests—handbooks. WM 34 F852h]
RC488.5.F73 1987 616.89'16 87-9417
ISBN 978-0-87630-466-2 (hbk)
ISBN 978-1-138-00947-9 (pbk)

We dedicate this Handbook
to the memory of our beloved parents
Neil and Clara Fredman
& David and Celia Sherman

Contents

Acknowledgments *xi*
Preface *xv*

CHAPTER 1. INTRODUCTION TO MARRIAGE AND FAMILY TESTING 3

CHAPTER 2. CLINICALLY POPULAR TESTS 17
Wechsler Intelligence Scale for Children-Revised and Wechsler Adult Intelligence Scale-Revised 17
Rorschach 18
Thematic Apperception Test 19
Draw-A-Person 19
House-Tree-Person 20
Minnesota Multiphasic Personality Inventory 20
Myers-Briggs Type Indicator 22
Strong-Campbell Interest Inventory of the Strong Vocational Interest Blank 22
Semantic Differential 23
Rokeach Value Survey 24

CHAPTER 3. OBSERVATIONAL MEASUREMENTS 27
MARITAL AND FAMILY INTERACTION CODING SYSTEM (MFICS) 29
CARD SORT PROCEDURE 31
BEAVERS-TIMBERLAWN FAMILY EVALUATION SCALE 33
FAMILY TASK INTERVIEW/FAMILY HEALTH SCALE 36

CHAPTER 4. GENERAL MARITAL SATISFACTION AND ADJUSTMENT SCALES 43
INTRODUCTION 43
1. MARITAL ADJUSTMENT TEST—LOCKE AND WALLACE 46
2. DYADIC ADJUSTMENT SCALE—SPANIER 52
3. MARITAL SATISFACTION SCALE: FORM B – ROACH, FRAZIER, AND BOWDEN 59
4. MARITAL SATISFACTION INVENTORY—SNYDER 65
5. MARITAL AGENDAS PROTOCOL—NOTARIUS AND VANZETTI 72
6. MCMASTER FAMILY ASSESSMENT DEVICE—EPSTEIN, BALDWIN, AND BISHOP 77
7. FAMILY ENVIRONMENT SCALE—MOOS AND MOOS 82
8. MARITAL ALTERNATIVES SCALE—UDRY 87
9. INVENTORY OF FAMILY FEELINGS—LOWMAN 91

CHAPTER 5. MARITAL COMMUNICATION AND INTIMACY SCALES 101
INTRODUCTION 101
10. MARITAL COMMUNICATION INVENTORY—BIENVENU 103
11. CARING RELATIONSHIP INVENTORY—SHOSTROM 106
12. ABBREVIATED BARRETT-LENNARD RELATIONSHIP INVENTORY—BARRETT-LENNARD, SCHUMM, BOLLMAN, AND JURICH 109
13. DYADIC TRUST SCALE—LARZELERE AND HUSTON 113
14. SELF-REPORT JEALOUSY SCALE-REVISED—BRINGLE 116
15. BORROMEAN FAMILY INDEX—BARDIS 122
16. WARING INTIMACY QUESTIONNAIRE—WARING 127

CHAPTER 6. SPECIAL FAMILY ASSESSMENT SCALES 131

INTRODUCTION 131

17. PRODUCTIVITY ENVIRONMENTAL PREFERENCE SURVEY—DUNN, DUNN, AND PRICE 134
18. ATTITUDES TOWARD FEMINISM SCALE—SMITH, FERREE, AND MILLER 141
19. ATTITUDES TOWARD WORKING WOMEN SCALE—TETENBAUM, LIGHTER, AND TRAVIS 145
20. DUAL-CAREER FAMILY SCALES—PENDLETON, POLOMA, AND GARLAND 150
21. MARITAL INSTABILITY SCALE—BOOTH AND EDWARDS 155
22. CONFLICT TACTICS SCALES—STRAUS 159
23. INTERPERSONAL BEHAVIOR SURVEY—MAUGER AND ADKINSON 164
24. FAMILY THERAPIST RATING SCALE—PIERCY, LAIRD, AND MOHAMMED 170

CHAPTER 7. MINNESOTA FAMILY INVENTORIES 177

INTRODUCTION 177

25. FAMILY ADAPTABILITY AND COHESION EVALUATION SCALES III—OLSON, PORTNER, AND LAVEE 180
26. QUALITY OF LIFE—OLSON AND BARNES 186
27. FAMILY STRENGTHS—OLSON, LARSEN, AND MCCUBBIN 191
28. FAMILY INVENTORY OF LIFE EVENTS AND CHANGES—MCCUBBIN, PATTERSON, AND WILSON 194
29. FAMILY CRISIS-ORIENTED PERSONAL EVALUATION SCALES—MCCUBBIN, OLSON, AND LARSEN 199
30. PREPARE-ENRICH INVENTORIES—FOURNIER, OLSON, AND DRUCKMAN 204
31. PERSONAL ASSESSMENT OF INTIMACY IN RELATIONSHIPS—OLSON AND SCHAEFER 210

CHAPTER 8. EPILOGUE 215

Acknowledgments

We are deeply indebted to many people for their assistance in the preparation of this book. We are particularly grateful to Leonore Hanson whose organizational skills and devotion made this book possible.

We wish to thank our secretary, Martha Hyber, for her excellent help.

It is a privilege to have been granted permission to quote the entire inventory or a part thereof from the copyrighted work of other authors. Their permission did not include direct collaboration or endorsement. The right of book purchasers or users to reproduce the inventories can be granted *only* by the inventory authors and publishers. A list of the quoted inventories follows in the order of appearance in the book:

Marital Adjustment Test from "Short marital adjustment and prediction tests: Their reliability and validity," by H. Locke and K. Wallace, in *Marriage and Family Living*, 1959, *2*, 251–255. Copyright 1959 by the National Council on Family Relations, 1910 West Country Road B, Suite 147, St. Paul, Minnesota 55113.* Reprinted by permission.

*For the sake of simplicity this address is cited only once, although the Council is acknowledged many times.

Dyadic Adjustment Scale from "Measuring dyadic adjustment: New scales for assessing the quality of marriage and similar dyads," by G. Spanier, in *Journal of Marriage and the Family*, 1976, *38*, 15-28. Copyright 1976 by the National Council on Family Relations. Reprinted by permission.

Marital Satisfaction Scale: Form B from "The Marital Satisfaction Scale: Development of a measure for intervention research," by A. Roach, L. Frazier, and S. Bowden, in *Journal of Marriage and the Family*, 1981, *41*, 537-545. Copyright 1981 by the National Council on Family Relations. Reprinted by permission.

Marital Satisfaction Inventory from *Marital Satisfaction Inventory (MSI) manual* by D. K. Snyder. Copyright © 1981 by Western Psychological Services. Not to be reproduced in whole or in part without written permission of Western Psychological Services. All rights reserved. Reprinted by permission of the publisher Western Psychological Services, 12031 Wilshire Blvd., Los Angeles, CA 90025.

Marital Agendas Protocol from "The Marital Agendas Protocol," by C. I. Notarius and N. A. Vanzetti in E. E. Filsinger (Ed.), *Marriage and family assessment: A sourcebook for family therapy*, 1983, 207-227. Beverly Hills, California: Sage Publications.

McMaster Family Assessment Device from "The McMaster Family Assessment Device," by N. Epstein, L. Baldwin, and S. Bishop, in *Journal of Marriage and Family Therapy*, 1983, *9*, 171-180.

Family Environment Scale from *Family Environment Scale manual* by R. H. Moos and B. S. Moos, 1981. Reproduced by special permission of the publisher, Consulting Psychologists Press, Inc. Palo Alto, California 94306.

Marital Alternatives Scale from "Marital alternatives and marital disruption," by R. Udry, in *Journal of Marriage and the Family*, 1981, *43*, 889-897. Copyright 1981 by the National Council on Family Relations. Reprinted by permission.

Inventory of Family Feelings, IFF Test Report, and Family Dyadic Relationships described by J. C. Lowman in "Measurement of family affective structure," in *Journal of Personality Assessment*, 1980, *44*, 130-141.

Caring Relationship Inventory from *Manual, Caring Relationship Inventory* by E. L. Shostrom, 1975. Reprinted by permission of publisher, EDITS/Educational and Industrial Testing Service, San Diego, California.

Abbreviated Barrett-Lennard Relationship Inventory from "Dimensionality of the Relationship Inventory: An urban replication with married couples," by W. R. Schumm, S. R. Bollman, and A. P. Jurich, in *Psychological Reports*, 1981, *48*, 51-56. Permission also granted by G. T. Barrett-Lennard.

Dyadic Trust Scale from "The Dyadic Trust Scale: Toward understanding interpersonal trust in close relationships," by R. Larzelere and T. Huston, in *Journal of Marriage and the Family*, 1980, *43*, 595-604. Copyright 1980 by the National Council on Family Relations. Reprinted by permission.

Self-Report Jealousy Scale—Revised described by R. Bringle, S. Roach, C. Andler, and S. Evenbeck in "Measuring the intensity of jealous reactions," in *Catalogue of Selected Documents in Psychology*, 1979, *9*, 23-24.

Borromean Family Index: For Single Persons and Borromean Family Index: For Married Persons from "The Borromean family," by P. D. Bardis, in *Social Science*, 1975, *50*, 144-158.

Productivity Environmental Preference Survey by R. Dunn, K. Dunn, and G. Price from *Productivity Environmental Survey manual* by G. Price, R. Dunn, and K. Dunn, 1982. Lawrence, KS: Price Systems, Inc.

Attitudes Toward Feminism Scale from "A Short Scale of Attitudes Toward Feminism," by E. R. Smith, M. M. Ferree, and F. D. Miller, in *Representative Research in Social Psychology*, 1975, *6*, 57-62.

Attitudes Toward Working Women Scale described by T. J. Tetenbaum, J. Lighter, and M. Travis in "Educators attitudes toward working mothers," in *Journal of Educational Psychology*, 1981, *73*, 369-375.

The Dual-Career Family Scales from "Scales for the investigation of the dual-career family," by B. F. Pendleton, M. M. Poloma, and T. N. Garland, in *Journal of Marriage and the Family*, 1980, *42*, 269-275. Copyright 1980 by the National Council on Family Relations. Reprinted by permission.

Marital Instability Scale and Short Marital Instability Scale from "Measuring marital instability," by A. Booth and J. Edwards, in *Journal of Marriage and the Family*, 1983, *45*, 387-393. Copyright 1983 by the National Council on Family Relations. Reprinted by permission.

Conflict Tactics Scales from "Measuring intrafamily conflict and violence: The Conflict Tactics (CT) Scales," by M. A. Straus, in *Journal of*

Marriage and the Family, 1979, *41*, 75-85. Copyright 1979 by the National Council on Family Relations. Reprinted by permission.

Interpersonal Behavior Survey by P. Mauger and D. Adkinson. Copyright © 1980 by Western Psychological Services. Excerpted from the *Interpersonal Behavior Survey* and reprinted by permission of the publisher, Western Psychological Services, 12031 Wilshire Blvd., Los Angeles, California 90025.

Family Therapist Rating Scale and Family Therapist Rating Scale Profile from "A Family Therapist Rating Scale," by F. Piercy, R. Laird, and Z. Mohammed, in *Journal of Marital and Family Therapy*, 1983, *9*, 49-59.

Family Adaptability and Cohesion Evaluation Scales III, by D. Olson, J. Portner, and Y. Lavee. In D. Olson, H. McCubbin, H. Barnes, A. Larsen, M. Muxen, and M. Wilson (Eds.), *Family inventories* (revised edition), 1985. St. Paul, MN: Family Social Science, University of Minnesota.

Quality of Life—Parent Form and Quality of Life—Adolescent Form by D. Olson and H. Barnes. In D. Olson et al., op. cit.

Family Strengths by D. Olson, A. Larsen, and H. McCubbin. In D. Olson et al., op. cit.

Family Inventory of Life Events and Changes by H. McCubbin, J. Patterson, and L. Wilson. In D. Olson et al., op. cit.

Family Crisis-Oriented Personal Evaluation Scales by H. McCubbin, A. Larsen, and D. Olson. In D. Olson et al., op. cit.

PREPARE-ENRICH from *PREPARE-ENRICH: Counselor's manual* by D. Olson, D. Fournier, and J. Druckman, 1982. Minneapolis: Prepare-Enrich Inc.

PAIR: Personal Assessment of Intimacy in Relationships by D. Olson and M. Schaefer (undated). St. Paul, MN: Family Social Services, University of Minnesota.

We owe our thanks to our editors, Ann Alhadeff and Natalie Gilman, for their invaluable guidance, assistance, and patience.

Preface

While running professional conferences and training programs for marriage and family therapists, we discovered a great demand for practical, efficient methods for gathering information and making diagnoses. Marriage and family inventories are increasingly available that can aid the working therapist, enlighten the student and intern, and provide reliable and valid measurements for researchers. Usually, these instruments can be found in professional journals.

Straus and Brown (1978) have listed and briefly described 813 marriage and family instruments published prior to 1975. Straus was astonished that so many instruments had been developed: "I thought there would be only 25 to 50 instruments in the literature." What this probably means is that marriage and family instruments were usually written for a specific research project and then abandoned. The language of testing, unfortunately, is the most technical in the field of psychology. Psychometrists, like modern poets, seem to write for each other.

But, fortunately, universities are demanding research from their clinical professors. Therefore, increasing numbers of therapist-researchers are developing instruments that go beyond the needs of a specific project and can be used by practitioners. We have gathered into this handbook four observational techniques and 31 of the more widely used paper-and-pencil instruments that have been published since 1975 (including one older "classic"). In addition, we have briefly discussed the marital and family implications of 11 very popular clinical tests and inventories. They are presented with respect for the demands of the psychometrist and the needs of the practitioner.

An effort has been made to minimize jargon. We wish to encourage therapists to use what are, in effect, "written techniques" to gather information, increase insight, and facilitate communication. Where jargon remains (for example, "dyadic" rather then "couple," "enmeshment" rather than "inappropriate overinvolvement"), the words are usually a gift from the field of therapy rather than the field of testing.

Marriage and family therapists are becoming more aware of the use and development of instruments because:

1. There is a desire to improve the objective, scientific bases of the profession.
2. The profession is trying to obtain government and public recognition of its competence and services, the accreditation of its practitioners, and the funding of grants.
3. Clinical professors working in university settings must meet the same rigorous proofs that are demanded of other health professions.
4. A growing number of clinicians have come to marriage and family therapy from individual therapy training, in which instrument usage has proven insightful and helpful.

The purpose of this handbook is to provide a single convenient source to which practitioners, researchers, and trainees can turn in order to learn how to use marriage and family instruments and to find descriptions of instruments suited to their needs. The instruments presented demonstrate the range of those available and tend to be the most widely quoted. The book is designed for quick reference. Readers may easily identify what they need by the category of measuring instrument.

Chapter 1 deals with the place of testing in marriage and family therapy, special testing problems in the field, the process of creating instruments, and how to use this handbook in selecting instruments.

Chapter 2 describes the most widely used tests and inventories in the fields of psychological counseling and therapy and how they might be used by marriage and family therapists.

Chapter 3 describes four of the most recently developed observational tools used to evaluate and diagnose family interaction.

Chapters 4 through 7 contain a compendium of measuring instruments. They list the tests available in the literature and some published works. For each instrument the handbook provides the title of the work, author(s), introduction, description of the instrument, description of the sample of people with whom the instrument was developed, reliability, validity, instructions to administer the inventory, where it can be located, and discussions on its use. Copies of the instruments are included if permission has been granted to do so. We cannot grant permission to copy any actual instrument; such permission can only be granted by authors and publishers.

Chapter 8 is an epilogue which identifies trends and needs in development of inventories in couple and family therapy.

The line between measurement and technique is not easy to draw. Indeed, we view measurement as one kind of technique. Textbooks on measurement often include some clinically respected, psychometrically criticized tools that appear in the *Handbook of Structured Techniques in Marriage and Family Therapy* (Sherman & Fredman, 1986). We recommend the following technique-measurements from that book:

- Technique 7 – Sentence Completion (pages 36–38)
- Technique 8 – Values Sentence Completion Form (pages 38–42)
- Technique 20 – The Genogram (pages 82–90)
- Technique 25 – The Family Sociogram (pages 109–114)

The choice of an instrument is based on theory and what is appropriate to the needs of the couple or family being seen. The more one uses an instrument (the same is true of any technique), the more one becomes aware of its strengths and weaknesses. We are very much aware that instrument results can be used as a tool to manipulate clients. Especially when issued as a computer printout, these results contain the aura of Science with a capital S. Since therapy in large part is designed to overcome resistance to change, the therapist needs to be sensitive to the ethics of testing as well as the ethics of using any effective technique. Ultimately, the interpretation becomes the instrument.

An ancient Chinese curse reads, "May you live through interesting times." That curse is unquestionably ours. It is our hope that this book will enable researchers and their students, therapists and their clients to gain insight into their lives and times.

N.F.
R.S.

REFERENCES

Sherman, R., & Fredman, N. (1986) *Handbook of structured techniques in marriage and family therapy*. New York: Brunner/Mazel.

Straus, M., & Brown, B. (1978) *Family measurement techniques: Abstracts of published instruments, 1935-1974*. Minneapolis: University of Minnesota Press.

Handbook of Measurements for Marriage and Family Therapy

1

Introduction to Marriage and Family Testing

Why do we need tests about marriage and families? As a matter of fact, we are testing informally all the time. The therapist asks questions and makes judgments at both the initial meeting and the subsequent meetings with the couple. After all, "What's going on?" is constantly being asked, silently or aloud. All right, then: Why do we need formal, objective tests about marriage and families? When Browning asked: "How do I love thee?/Let me count the ways," she did not come up with a T-score and a standard error of measurement.

The question implies that there is something chilling about the very touch of testing that makes it inappropriate to marital warmth—inflexible plastic in a world of skin. It is true that tests are used in schools, but even there they can interfere with a close relationship between teacher and child. Can you see Carl Rogers sneaking a look at a child's IQ score? If Goldman (1972) can speak of an uneasy marriage between testing and *school* counseling, what would he say of testing and marriage therapy?

Formal testing is usually appropriate in institutions like the army or big business where the institution is ignorant about the test taker, relates to him* in a formal manner, and affords him opportunities of promotion and change based on test results. Even schools can follow this three-point model: ignorance about the test taker, objective formal relations, and an opportunity for promotion or change. But surely not marriages. Husbands and wives, parents and children know everything worthwhile knowing about each other. Indeed, the Bible even calls the intimacy between husband and wife "knowledge." Family relationships are warm. And marriage is forever.

Ignorance

At one level, questionnaires can be useful to eliminate fantasies about one's mate. The low correlations between husbands' and wives' scores on measures of family adaptability and cohesion (Olson et al., 1985) might mean that they do not know what the family looks like in the eyes of their mates. Dunn and Dunn (1978) have found that couples in 72 intact marriages had a tendency to have quite different environmental preferences in such important, yet ignored, areas as keeping the room warm or cool, light or dark, noisy or quiet, organized or "lived in." It may have always been so. Even nursery rhymes speak of the complementarity necessary to keep thin Jack Sprat and his corpulent wife efficient. Awareness of all differences for many couples can increase tolerance of those differences.

Formality

Some marriages are too informal without being warm. There are moments in a relationship in which objectivity can be a step towards better communication and ultimately more warmth.

Change

Nowadays, the possibilities of radical changes in the family not only can affect the husband-wife relationship but the parent-child relationship as

*For the sake of simplicity, unless the therapist or client is obviously identifiable by sex, the therapist will be referred to by the female pronoun and the client by the male pronoun.

well. Legally, a child can literally gain a new mother or father. Of course, on a less drastic level, change is what family therapy is about. Formal testing is now appropriate for families in distress and families that would like to avoid distress.

To the degree that marriage therapy can be taught, that progress is possible, that the next generation of therapists can learn from us (or at least from our mistakes), to the degree that marriage therapy is a science rather than an art, some answer must be attempted to the question "Does therapy work?" Objective formal testing tries to answer that question: Has the therapy had any effect? Insurance payments and court decisions mean that effectiveness of treatment will require more than clinical assertion.

Edward Thorndike's statement "That which cannot be measured may not exist" seems a bit extreme, and we are tempted to respond, "That which can be measured may be irrelevant." Yet the reality of self-delusion that we spot so well in others just might infect us as well. Measurement can put some limits on subjectivity and open the practitioner to alternative therapeutic techniques. It can help identify the problem, providing a quick and efficient first screening. Hours of interview time can be saved by appropriate measurement. Sometimes tests can even monitor the improvement or deterioration of family relationships while it is happening. Even when the test as a whole lacks respectable reliability and validity, individual items can suggest clinical questions and techniques that can influence the family relationship.

We live increasingly in a multimedia environment. However, much of therapy is an auditory experience. One of the purposes of our volume, *Handbook of Structured Techniques in Marriage and Family Therapy*, (Sherman & Fredman, 1986) was to add visual, kinesthetic, and tactile dimensions to the therapy session. It is important not to dismiss a test printout as "just intellectual." It is a visual experience that often inspires confidence not granted to the spoken word. And by comparing the family's results with the results of a sample of other families, the family can move beyond the myth of uniqueness. At the very least, many clients view a properly administered and interpreted inventory as "doing something" about the marriage conflict.

Problems of Marriage and Family Inventories

Measuring marriage is not quite like measuring reading. Cronbach (1984) made the distinction between trying to measure best performance and trying to measure typical performance. Some people advocate reserving the word "test" for measures of best performance. They use words like "scale," "inventory," or "questionnaire" for measures of typical performance.

A paper-and-pencil test has a tough enough time trying to rate a group of students trying to do their best. Personality evaluations usually demand honesty and insight that may be lacking in the general population, let alone among emotionally involved clients.

If someone ran pupil responses to an arithmetic test through a computer, she would probably find that all the questions were measuring the same thing: arithmetic. If someone were to run client responses to an anxiety questionnaire through a computer, however, she would probably *not* find that all the questions were measuring the same thing. Or she might find that they were measuring the same thing that could not really be labeled "anxiety."

Some people, when given the choice of rating feelings, refuse to check extreme scores, like "always" or "never"; others check extreme scores regularly. Some people tend to agree with attitudinal questions with surprisingly little regard for their contents; other provocative souls disagree with the same disregard for the actual content.

Even assuming that the people filling out questionnaires are cooperative, honest, and insightful and do not have the habit of answering questions in a given pattern that slightly ignores well-thought-out directions, it is still technically difficult to total personality-based items into a score. The goal of a chemistry test is to get 100. The goal on any question is to get it right. Test makers can make sure to throw out any item on which unsuccessful students for some reason (like guessing or ambiguity) did better than successful students.

But take a test about anxiety or assertiveness or marital cohesion. Who says that a perfect score is ideal? A high score in cohesion may signal an enmeshment problem rather than good adjustment. Just as a perfect score on the total test is not desirable, it is not necessarily desirable to answer any single item "correctly." Two people who produce the same cohesion score may have checked very different items. The relationship between two items is such that you cannot say that those who answered yes to one item will tend to answer yes to another item. If items do not function in such a way, it becomes hard to compute a total score that has much meaning.

It is extremely difficult to measure change scores, even when measuring knowledge (Thorndike & Hagen, 1978). It is even harder to measure change of individual emotions, and therapists are not interested in selection and description; they are interested precisely in change—emotional and behavioral change.

Thus it happens that not only are practitioners afraid that the use of tests can cool therapist-client relationships, but also researchers are afraid that personality measurements may be giving bogus answers to the important questions "Does therapy work?" and "What changes should be made?"

In addition, marriage inventories present a unique problem. The body to be measured is not the individual or even the group; it is the system and the relationships. Tests, by the definition used by test makers, are essentially measures of individual differences. Tests are written and rewritten to maximize the consistency of differences between individuals and to demonstrate that the difference has some meaning or use. When group scores are used, these individuals' scores are averaged and the spread of scores described in a popularly agreed-upon fashion. But you cannot simply average a wife-and-husband's score. We suppose you could if you were interested in their average weight to predict wear-and-tear on furniture. But if you are interested in the relationships, in the system, an average score, even accompanied by statements about how the wife differs from the husband, will not suffice.

The closest thing that now exists to a survey that measures systems are Classroom Interaction Scales. An outside observer marks (usually once every three seconds) who in the class said or did what to whom. Was the statement a question or a response, emotionally positive or negative, directed to a student, a peer, or the teacher? Modifications of this technique are not appropriate for marriage and family therapy, except, perhaps, by training institutions evaluating counselor trainees. For one thing, an outsider can sit in the back of a room without being too obtrusive when one teacher and 25 students are learning algebra. But when a therapist and a couple are discussing alcohol abuse, how unobtrusive can an outsider be? Moreover, the classroom observed is the arena being evaluated when we measure classroom interaction. Except when we are measuring the therapeutic relationship, the observed therapy session is usually *not* what we really want to evaluate in family therapy; we usually want to measure the family system outside the therapy session.

Observational techniques have been reported by Filsinger (1983a,b). These techniques generally require special equipment and special training to improve a commonly reported fault: low agreement between observers. For first-time users, the authors of the Couples Interaction Scoring System " . . . estimate that it can take 24 hours to code an hour of videotape" (Filsinger, 1983b, p. 126). Videotape for therapy insight is increasingly used and is described as a technique in the *Handbook of Structured Techniques in Marriage and Family Therapy* (pp. 198, 233–236). As a practical measurement tool, observational techniques await a breakthrough in efficiency. (Chapter 2 of this book will briefly describe some of these observational systems.)

The measurements included in this volume are self-report questionnaires dealing with values, attitudes, adjustment problems, and crisis management. All but one of the inventories we discuss are less than a decade old. On the negative side, this means that most have not had time to develop a history of successful clinical use. On the positive side, this means that the authors have had the technical advantage of using computers and the practical advantage of decades of testing and family therapy research.

How Inventories Are Made

Although the vast majority of marriage and family inventories located by Straus and Brown (1978) were constructed to answer a specific research problem, inventories increasingly are made to help the clinician. Nevertheless, universities remain the major source of new inventories. When family centers are associated with universities or church organizations, or are desirous of government funds, these centers must prove that they are effective.

When a presenting problem arises consistently at the family center such as wife abuse or quarrels over child rearing, or a grant has been funded, some clinicians may suggest using a questionnaire to expedite intake interviews, enlighten clients, or monitor therapeutic progress. A computer search through the literature may be disappointing for various reasons. Marriage and family therapy is such a rapidly expanding field that the available inventories might be inconsistent with the theoretical framework of the center. It might be felt that certain specific areas crucial to the needs of the clients have not been thoroughly covered.

If a new paper-and-pencil questionnaire needs to be constructed, the authors will first collect statements from the literature that are consistent with both their theoretical framework and their information-gathering needs. Hundreds of statements will be gathered. Then they will be rewritten in a style that is very readable. Seventh grade vocabulary is the goal. Jargon is weeded out. All statements are usually rewritten in a similar form. "Experts" will evaluate the statements for readability and appropriateness. If the questionnaire is long, a true-false or yes-no answering format will be used. A shorter questionnaire can use what is similar to a multiple choice format. There are often five choices varying from "always" to "never" or from "strongly agree" to "strongly disagree."

In questionnaire construction, the easiest step to describe is the hardest to do: obtain a representative sample, first to try out the inventory, then to serve as a comparison group. This is a weak spot in every test. The sample is made up of volunteers, and volunteers tend to be nonrepresentative. Kinsey discovered this when he reported that his sample of men had more sex with women than his sample of women had with men (Kinsey et al., 1948, 1953). The samples used by achievement tests number in the tens of thousands. Yet even these samples are so nonrepresentative that clever superintendents can change the results of their pupils simply by switching to a test that uses a different population as a comparison group.

For the first run-throughs a truly random or even representative sample is unnecessary. The authors just need to find the items that are not "functioning." Marriage and family inventories tend to use students and their willing friends meeting a class assignment.

The next step sounds very difficult, but thanks to the computer is actually quite simple (and fantastically impressive): run an item analysis. The authors "tell" the computer to select the items that "go together," that usually produce the same results as the total inventory. The assumption is that the total inventory is closer to the truth than any single item. Those items that do not "function" (that do not produce the same results as the total inventory) are identified. In baseball, a line drive can be just an impressive out; a strikeout is an embarrassment. Managers will yank the players who strike out and try again with the players who line the ball. The computer can only tell the authors which items made the outs. At first, the authors will probably throw out almost all the items that do not function. But even after the first tryout, they will start slightly modifying the language of items they really like. They may even try it again unchanged, blaming the first failure on the umpire. ("The sample used may have been improper.")

The authors must try again. If they simply report the results of the original tryout using only the items that work, it is a little like computing one's batting average without the strikeouts. The second time, of course, a different sample would be used. If there is to be no third tryout, this second sample must be as representative as the authors can make it.

By the final trial the inventory authors must answer the following questions:

1. Will two or more judges agree about the score assigned to any individual or family? This is one of the reasons that paper-and-pencil tests are so popular and observational scales so difficult to construct.

2. Will the items of an inventory or of a subtest "go together" so that the total inventory or subtest scores can be used? Five cows and five boys do not make 10 cowboys. If the items do not go together (technically, if they lack "internal consistency"), the individual items may be useful, but the total score is useless. Reliability scores between .80 and .90 are the goal.

3. Will the total scores remain stable over time? The inventory will probably be administered (in its final form) to the same group twice, with an interim period of two to six weeks. If the scores change in a brief time—without therapy—it becomes impossible to use the instrument to tell if the therapy has had any effect.

4. Can the inventory distinguish between stable and unstable families? The unstable family may be divorced or approaching divorce. At the very least, any measure of family satisfaction should be able

to distinguish between the two. The unstable family may have a seriously disturbed member (called the identified patient or I.P.). Will the inventory distinguish between families with such problems and those without?

5. Will inventory results be consistent with the theory on which the inventory is based? The schizophrenogenic mother is a common feature of family literature. Yet families with schizophrenic children score "better" than families with neurotic children. Families that ignore the traditional stereotypical husband-wife roles are "in"—except on inventory results. Complementarity is "in"—except on inventory results. Perhaps the theories need to be somewhat modified; or perhaps, the inventories.

Factor analysis is so easy to do with computers that it is almost required. The authors put the responses of a few hundred respondents into the computers and see which items go with each other. If all items go together (except a few that can be discarded), the instrument has one factor. When the instrument has two or more factors, the test maker now must use creativity as well as the computer. By reading the items that go together, the test maker can evoke a name that seems to describe that collection of items. But caution needs to be taken. Items can go together not because their content is similar, but because their style is similar.

For example, Family Strengths is a 12-item instrument from the respected pens of David Olson, Andrea Larsen, and Hamilton McCubbin. (Olson et al., 1985). Factor analysis revealed two factors in this inventory: one labeled "pride," the other labeled "accord" (family sense of mastery). But it just might be that the two factors are the product of the positive language of the factor ("We are proud of our family") and the negative language of the second factor ("We are critical of each other").

Factor analysis, then, only tells you that clients respond to one set of statements differently than they do to another set of statements. The reason why they differ is left to private judgment and public argument. Factor analysis should be used when the authors claim the instrument possesses two or more subscales in order to determine if indeed there are that many scales and if the items have been properly assigned.

The Review Pattern in this Handbook

Each review of an instrument in this book consists of: 1) an *introduction*, 2) a *description* of the instrument, 3) a description of the *sample* used to develop the instrument, 4) a report on *reliability*, 5) a report on *validity*, 6) a procedure section telling how to *administer* the instrument, 7) a *location* section (where to read more about the instrument), 8) a *discussion* section, and 9) a list of any *references* quoted. Sample items—or, where possible, the entire test—are included after the review.

1. The *introduction* briefly describes the inventory. A line or two will recite the underlying concepts the instrument is trying to measure. Then the length and style of the inventory is reported.

2. The *description* reports how the questions were written, refined, and selected. The various sections of the instrument are described and sometimes sample items are quoted. This section becomes very important when the whole test or substantial sections cannot be quoted because of copyright laws.

3. The *sample* describes the group that served for reliability and validity studies and served as the comparison group. Let users beware of inventories whose sample come from the student body of one university. Students and their willing friends meeting a class assignment do not constitute a representative sample. Other inventories are based on the responses of church groups. The cooperation of church groups is wonderful, but there may be areas in which church members do not answer like nonchurch members.

Sampling will remain a problem. The best that can be hoped for is a well-described sample that, though not random, at least represents the various developmental stages in the marriages of several geographic, ethnic, religious, and socioeconomic groups.

4. The *reliability* section is more technical than the others. Unfortunately, the reliability must be reported as a number rather than merely described. People are never consistent enough to produce reliability coefficients of a perfect 1.00. However, if the consistency gets too low, the total score cannot be used. Reliabilities above .90 are excellent but

suspect. Reliabilities above .80 are all right. Reliabilities below .70 mean that the results can be used only for group research. There are ways of falsely inflating reliability coefficients. Computing reliabilities on a wildly disparate group of divorcing and happily married couples will report a consistency of differences that will probably disappear on a random group of married couples. This inflated reliability may not present a problem when measuring clients who are coming for therapy. It can present a problem when dealing with couples attending a marriage enrichment program.

One central reliability problem is created by the brevity of subscales. As any beginning text on testing notes, the longer the instrument the more internally consistent are the results. A simple formula (Spearman–Brown Prophecy Formula [see Cronbach, 1984, p. 171]) predicts that a 100-item instrument with a highly respectable reliability of .91 will become a 10-item scale with an unusable reliability of .50. Clinicians prefer the short 10-item scale to the laborious 100-item inventory; indeed, 100-item inventories are typically broken down into 10 subscales to get 10 different kinds of information. Alas, it cannot be done. Some of the most appealing inventories offer tempting information that must be stamped as scientifically unsound. This reliability-versus-fascination dilemma has not been solved.

5. The *validity* section describes the usefulness and meaning of the inventory. Typically, marriage questionnaires rely on the obvious content of the items, technically called face validity. But it is one thing to say that the ability to answer a question about multiplication reflects mastery of fifth grade curriculum; it is another matter entirely to say that to give a socially approved response to a question about human communication reflects mastery of human relationships.

Most test makers quoted in this book try to validate their instrument by showing an ability to discriminate between families who have come in for therapy and families who seem reasonably intact. Few demonstrate an ability to predict who will have trouble. Many instruments validate themselves by comparing results with other instruments. When IQ test makers say that their inexpensive paper-and-pencil test produces the same results as the costly Wechsler Intelligence Scale for Children (WISC), it makes sense—at least economic sense—to use the inexpensive brand. But when validity is claimed for a marriage inventory because it correlates significantly with the inexpensive, paper-and-pencil Locke-Wallace—well, why not use the Locke-Wallace (see Measure #1)?

6. The *administration* of most of the instruments is usually untimed and the grading is usually done by hand. If the instrument is computer-scored, there is generally a wait of two weeks for the return of the computer printout before the inventory can be interpreted. Unless specifically stated otherwise, the couple or family should respond as individuals without knowing how the other has responded until after the inventory has been completed. Of course, the individuals should be informed that their responses will be shared with others if that is what will indeed be done.

Some general suggestions for administering the instruments are:

(a) The administrator should take the instrument first to become familiar with it before giving it to anyone else.

(b) It is generally preferable for all members to take the instrument at the same time in the office or clinic to avoid discussion prior to responding to the items. However, some inventories can be taken at home to save time in session, such as F-COPES described in Chapter 7.

(c) Give the instructions as they are written, so that the instrument is used as the authors intended.

(d) Have all necessary materials available.

7. The *location* of the article, book, or manual that has provided the reported information is given.

8. A *discussion* section usually completes the report. Research results may be included, especially when the research tells of new populations or uses for the instrument. The strengths and weaknesses of the instrument are briefly examined. Sometimes the test authors have suggested practical ways to use the instrument.

Obviously, the most important part of using an instrument is the interpretation of the data obtained. What do they all mean? How can the data be applied to the process of behavior change? The inventory author provides the rationale for the inventory and the definitions of the terms and concepts used. Other levels of interpretation are as follows:

(a) Comparisons can be made with other couples or families in the inventory reference group.

(b) The information can be fed into the theoretical model favored by the therapist to give further meaning to it.

(c) The data are examined in the light of cultural and subcultural values.

(d) The meaning of the responses are checked out in relation to the myths and beliefs of the members individually and as a family—their internal framework of meaning.

9. *References* quoted in the report are listed. Other references can be located by examining the bibliography of the main article, book, or manual.

The instrument itself is sometimes quoted in part or in full. No permission can be given by us to copy any instrument, since we are not the authors of these instruments. Readers are urged to observe copyright laws and contact authors and publishers if they intend to use the instruments.

It is necessary to use technical terms in the reliability and validity sections. Both reliability and validity are necessary components of an instrument for the therapist as well as the researcher to examine.

Testing and Techniques

Tests generally aim for a precise measurement that enables the test user to make a wise selection based on perfect prediction. This is really a soothsayer model. When the weather forecaster predicts rain in the afternoon, you take your umbrella along even when the morning sky is clear blue. We do not change the weather; we change our reaction to it. The prophetic model is different. If Nineveh goes on its merry way, disaster looms. But Nineveh can repent. Physicians and therapists use this prophetic model: if things continue as they have been, trouble looms; if things change, trouble can disappear. Especially in the case of marriage instruments, measurements that lack predictive powers can still serve as motivators of thought, insight, and communication. Thus marriage instruments can be used as techniques even when they lack the reliability and validity that we might prefer. The *Handbook of Structured Techniques in Marriage and Family Therapy* (Sherman & Fredman, 1986) actually contains techniques (Sentence Completion, Values Clarification, and the Family Sociogram) that could, with more intensive data collecting, be treated as inventories.

REFERENCES

Cronbach, L. (1984). *Essentials of psychological testing* (4th edition). New York: Harper & Row.

Dunn, K., & Dunn, R. (1978). Comparison of adult learning styles in intact marriages (unpublished manuscript).

Filsinger, E. (1983a). Implication in the choice of marital observations coding system: A user's guide. *Family Process, 22* (3), 317-326.

Filsinger, E. (1983b). *Marriage and family assessment.* Beverly Hills: Sage.

Goldman, L. (1972). Tests and counseling: The marriage that failed. *Measurement and Evaluation in Guidance, 4*, 213-220.

Kinsey, A., Pomeroy, B., & Martin, C. (1948). *Sexual behavior in the human male.* Philadelphia: W. B. Saunders.

Kinsey, A., & others. (1953). *Sexual behavior in the human female.* Philadelphia: W. B. Saunders.

Olson, D., McCubbin, H., Barnes, H., Larsen, A., Maxen, M., & Wilson, M. (1985). *Family inventories* (revised edition). St. Paul: Family Social Science.

Straus, M., & Brown, B. (1978). *Family measurement techniques: Abstracts of published instruments, 1935-1974.* Minneapolis: University of Minnesota Press.

Sherman, R., & Fredman, N. (1986). *Handbook of structured techniques in marriage and family therapy.* New York: Brunner/Mazel.

Thorndike, R., & Hagen, E. (1978). *Measurement and evaluation in psychology and education* (4th edition). New York: John Wiley & Sons.

2
Clinically Popular Tests

We believe that among those tests most widely used by therapists are IQ tests, the Rorschach, the Thematic Apperception Test, the Draw-A-Person Test, the House-Tree-Person, and the Minnesota Multiphasic Personality Inventory. Counselors might add the Myers-Briggs Type Indicator and various vocational and value inventories. Researchers might add the Semantic Differential. Of course, these tests and inventories are intended for individuals rather than family systems. By considering in this chapter some of these well-known tests, we wish to remind therapists that insights into the family can be gained through widely used "nonfamily" tests and inventories.

WECHSLER INTELLIGENCE SCALE FOR CHILDREN-REVISED AND WECHSLER ADULT INTELLIGENCE SCALE-REVISED

Certain items in the Wechsler Intelligence Scale for Children-Revised (WISC-R) (Wechsler, 1974) and Wechsler Adult Intelligence Scale-Revised (WAIS-R) (Wechsler, 1981) are relevant to the family. The

Picture Arrangement subtest of the WAIS-R contains five items (the subtest is only 10 items long) that concern male-female role interactions. In three cases (the problems labeled "Flirt," "Romeo," and "Taxi"), the traditional male-female interaction is part of the knowledge needed to arrange the pictures correctly. In two cases, the male-female roles have been reversed: In the problem labeled "Hill," a woman pulls a man up the hill after he has failed to pull her up; in the problem labeled "Escape," a male convict steals a woman's clothing, but ironically she is an escaping convict, too. The Picture Arrangement subtest in the WISC-R no longer pictures the wife nagging her husband to garden or to carry an umbrella; now, the scene involves mothers and children. These items like the question, "Why does the state require people to get a license before they get married?" are basically part of the effort to measure the individual's verbal and nonverbal cognitive strengths, but the responses can provide insights into the family dynamics.

RORSCHACH

Rorschach couple interpretation is available (Dudek, 1954; Dudek & Gottlieb, 1954) but not widely given, perhaps because the Rorschach is traditionally used by those who emphasize intrapsychic insight rather than family systems.

The Number 4 card of the Rorschach has been called the Father card because of the common perception of a tall giant. The Number 6 card is thought to reveal attitudes towards sex because of a common perception of male and female genitals. The Number 7 card has been called the Mother card because of its common perception of a cave or cradle. The more recent interpretations of the Rorschach emphasize the client's style of response more than the content. How does the client use color, form, wholes, details, motion, shading, and vista? What was the reaction time? This style of interpretation may be less poetic and more quantifiable than interpretation of context, but, at present, it has little relevance for marriage counseling and therapy.

Rorschach group testing has been developed but usually for the purpose of speeding up the testing time, not as a means of understanding the group as a system. Loveland, Wynne, and Singer (1963) and Levy and Epstein (1964), however, have described ways of using the

Rorschach with an entire family, after testing family members individually in the traditional fashion.

THEMATIC APPERCEPTION TEST

The Thematic Apperception Test (TAT) is another commonly used projective inventory. Clients are shown a slightly ambiguous picture with the direction to tell a story. Several cards evoke family stories. Card 2 shows a woman in the foreground with books in her hand. In the background a man is working in the fields with an older woman looking on. This farm scene usually conjures up a story concerning family relationships and aspirations. Card 3 shows a figure, supposedly a boy, with his head bowed on his right arm. There is a revolver on the floor beside him. This card calls forth stories of severe emotional disturbance often involving family and loved ones. Several other cards evoke stories about relationship between the sexes, with parents with guilt or involving stereotyped sex roles. Even the totally blank card has a tendency to evoke family stories. The TAT has been used by Jay Haley (1964) who developed a method of observing families telling a story based on TAT cards. A machine tabulated the interaction between mother, father, and child. The rigidity of the interaction sequence rather than the story content was used to indicate pathology.

DRAW-A-PERSON

The Draw-A-Person (D-A-P) (Harris, 1963) has gained respect as a nonverbal measure of intelligence. When used as a personality inventory, testing critics find considerable fault with the D-A-P, while clinicians love it. Does the absence of feet in a drawing really mean insecurity? Recent studies seem to indicate that a more global approach has more validity than the limb-by-limb approach.

Sarrell, Sarrell, and Berman (1981) have demonstrated the use of the Draw-A-Person for sex and couple therapy. Each family member is asked to draw with a pencil on a standard unlined sheet of paper a picture of a person—"The best picture of a person you can draw." When the drawing is completed, a fresh sheet of paper is handed to the client, who is asked to draw the best picture of a person of the opposite sex to the person first drawn. Now each client has drawn a man and a woman and the two pairs of drawings can be compared for maturity, anger, sexuality, and even size. Sarrell administers the Draw-A-Person to couples before, during, and after therapy, and changes in the drawings can sometimes be startling.

HOUSE-TREE-PERSON

The House-Tree-Person (Hammer, 1980) adds two drawings to the Draw-A-Person Test—four, if the drawing is done first with pencil, then with crayon. The house drawing is thought to arouse associations concerning home life and intrafamilial relations. Whether the family described is the family of origin or the present spouse is a problem the therapist must answer. The chimney drawing may reveal psychosexual conflict; heavy smoke may reveal a hot and turbulent home environment; the door and windows are interpreted as revealing attitudes to contact with the environment. The tree symbolizes life and growth and is said to reflect relatively deeper and more unconscious feelings about one's self. Drawings of branches reflect the subject's search for satisfaction from the environment. Children's drawings of branches reaching for the sun are thought to signify marked and frustrated needs for affection.

Robert Burns (1987) has developed Kinetic Family Drawing as a projective measurement. The entire family participates following the instruction to make a unified House-Tree-Person drawing with some action.

No groups of tests create as much conflict in the field of testing as do projective tests. The clinicians' awe is matched by the psychometrists' contempt. Users beware.

MINNESOTA MULTIPHASIC PERSONALITY INVENTORY

The computer and the intake interview have done much to revive the Minnesota Multiphasic Personality Inventory (MMPI). The MMPI is an objective multidimensional inventory used to assist in the identification of psychopathology. Its 550 different items require a true or false response.

Scale 4 (traditionally called "Psychopathic Deviate") relates to family conflicts. This is not surprising when one realizes that many of its items refer to conflict with parents. MMPI results are intended to be interpreted in patterns. That is, the clinician does not simply note that scale 4 is high. She must also note what other scales are high.

A high 2–4 (the 2 scale was traditionally called "Depression") is most commonly found among those evaluated by the courts for a crime. They are typically hostile, resentful, and immature reacting to stress by substance abuse and are given to self-pity and blaming others. A high 3–4 (the 3 scale was traditionally called "Hysteria") tends to be passive-aggressive. If the 4 is higher, there may be sudden explosions of rage. Typically, marital discord is accompanied by sexual maladjustment, attempts to dominate, and the conversion of therapy sessions into complaints about others. A high 4–5 (the 5 scale was traditionally called "Masculinity-Femininity") is found among women rebelling against the feminine role, while maintaining strong needs for dependency. A high 4–6 (the 6 scale was traditionally called "Paranoia") is associated with excessive demands for attention and with substance abuse. A high 4–7 (the 7 scale was traditionally called "Psychasthenia") is found among those who have patterns of sexual promiscuity and drug abuse followed by periods of guilt and remorse. A high 4–8 (the 8 scale was traditionally called "Schizophrenia") indicates limited ability to express emotions in an appropriate way and serious sexual identity concerns. Clients with high 4–9 scores (the 9 scale was traditionally called "Hypomania") tend to be impulsive and irresponsible. They rarely try therapy.

As even this superficial review should indicate, the MMPI is a subtle and complicated instrument. In the 1960s, unions pressured Congress into forbidding government funds for its use. The computer has revived the MMPI, but an easy-to-read printout increases the need for caution, even when statements are not contradictory (as sometimes happens). The group with whom the client is compared is generally seriously disturbed. Personality inventories like the MMPI that do not integrate what the therapist knows or can learn about the client have a poor validity record.

MYERS-BRIGGS TYPE INDICATOR

The *Myers-Briggs Type Indicator* (Briggs & Myers, 1977) is probably the most widely used personality and counseling instrument for "normal" populations. It was first published in 1943. A revised, shortened version in 1983 brought a resurgence of use, especially by business organizations. Jung's theory of type underlies the Myers-Briggs; it was Jung, after all, who stressed complementarity in marital relations. We marry someone to provide what our own personalities lack. Jung had developed a simple projective test to measure the individual's masculine and feminine characteristics: two overlapping triangles (what most of us would recognize as the Star of David). This simple test never caught on.

The *Myers-Briggs* tries to sort individuals into four separate dichotomies, of which the best known is Extroversion-Introversion. People are also divided by their ways of finding out about the world around them: Sensing (fact-oriented) and Intuitive. There are two ways of deciding: Thinking and Feeling. And there are two ways of acting: orderly or spontaneously, a dichotomy *Myers-Briggs* names Judgment-Perception.

Insight into the other person's type is meant to enhance understanding and communication. Opposites (sometimes) attract and if they understand the attraction, this is well and good. However, if each party tries to change the other, conflict arises when the "reform" is not successful. Ironically, if somehow each party were successful in changing the other, the dissimilar typology would, of course, remain.

The *Myers-Briggs* manual (Briggs-Myers & McCauley, 1985) quotes research to show that complementarity is not quite as common in "happily" married couples as is similarity. However, insight about the significant people in our lives can enhance relationships whether the other is similar or different.

STRONG-CAMPBELL INTEREST INVENTORY OF THE STRONG VOCATIONAL INTEREST BLANK

The Strong-Campbell Interest Inventory (Hansen, 1984; Strong, Campbell, & Hansen, 1985) asks the client to respond "like," "indifferent," or "dislike" to 325 activities, groups of people, or characteristics.

The results are then compared with the results of men and women in over 100 occupations. These occupations are categorized by Holland's (1973) theory as: Realistic (or skilled labor), Investigative (or scientific), Artistic, Social, Enterprising, and Conventional (or office work). These six vocational types are placed in order around a hexagon. Those vocational choices in or next to the area chosen by the client are areas of greatest similarity. For example, artists would share interests with those who work with people, with scientists, and, of course, with other artists. The artists would be most dissimilar to office workers, and would usually share few interests with skilled laborers and enterprising businessmen.

Bruch and Skovholt (1985) found that only 5% of a group of distressed couples could be characterized as having similar vocations. More than half the nondistressed couples investigated had vocations in common. Bruch and Skovholt compared the actual vocation in which the husband and wife were employed. However, the same logic that shared interests lead to marital happiness should hold true when these interests are measured by commonly used inventories. Examination of interests could be important to premarital and marital therapy. But marriage therapists should not make the error sometimes made by vocational counselors: do not emphasize the specific profession; do emphasize the six areas in which these professions can be categorized.

SEMANTIC DIFFERENTIAL

The Semantic Differential (Osgood, Suci, & Tannenbaum, 1957) can be used in marital assessment. A word or concept is placed on top of a page, such as "Me" or "Abortion" or "My Spouse." Then a series of word pairs is placed beneath the concept. As illustrated (p. 24), usually seven blank spaces are placed between the pair of words to measure the degree to which the respondent describes the concept under question.

Research reports three main dimensions of meaning (Osgood, Suci, & Tannenbaum, 1957): evaluation, strength, and activity. Thus a client might report his mother as very good and moderately affectionate (evaluation words), very strong and very capable (strength words), and moderately passive and slightly energetic (activity words). The ease with which this instrument can be constructed means that it is inexpen-

Example of the Semantic Differential

For *each pair* of words, put one and only one "X" in the space that best describes how the words relate to your spouse.

MY SPOUSE

	VERY	MODERATELY	SLIGHTLY	EQUALLY	SLIGHTLY	MODERATELY	VERY	
Good	___	___	___	___	___	___	___	Bad
Affectionate	___	___	___	___	___	___	___	Cold
Strong	___	___	___	___	___	___	___	Weak
Helpless	___	___	___	___	___	___	___	Capable
Passive	___	___	___	___	___	___	___	Active
Energetic	___	___	___	___	___	___	___	Lazy

sive, quick, and easy. Representative comparison groups are not available and some critics believe that responses are superficial and purely verbal, but that is a danger in most paper-and-pencil assessments of attitude. The clinician, however, should bear in mind these three main dimensions that research has consistently discovered.

Despite the absence of any representative group with which to compare the family, comparisons are made clinically between respondents (for example, comparing how husband and wife see "Women's Liberation"). Comparisons are also made between concepts (for example, comparing responses to "Me" and "How My Wife Sees Me").

Some individuals give extreme responses and others moderate responses regardless of the specific question asked: for example, a husband who rates his wife's virtues moderately may be reflecting his own inability to evaluate anything or anyone strongly.

ROKEACH VALUE SURVEY

Differences in values might be a source of conflict. Rokeach (1973) has developed a widely used Value Survey of 18 goals (called "terminal values") and 18 ways of reaching those goals (called "instrumental values"). The six most popular terminal values of a sample of American men in order of preference were a world at peace, family security, freedom, a comfortable life, happiness, and self-respect. The sample of American women placed salvation fourth and a comfortable life thirteenth, almost reversing the positions these values had for the men. Significant differences were also reported on the instrumental values of ambitious (second for men, fourth for women), capable (eighth for men, twelfth for women), forgiving (sixth for men, second for women), and loving (fourteenth for men, ninth for women). Like other value instruments, the Rokeach Value Survey avoids judgments about a person's choices. It is interesting to take, brief to complete, and relatively easy to process. It requires at least a high school education to take. The stability of rankings is modest, leading to the possible conclusion that value systems, at least as measured by this survey, are not deep and long-lasting. With caution such instruments might be used in premarital counseling or to discover sources of conflict in the family.

All the instruments we have discussed in this chapter are directed towards the individual rather than the family system. Comparison of a husband's and wife's interests, values, and personalities can shed some light on family interaction. Difference scores, however, should not be exaggerated. After all, sometimes you can differ with *yourself* on an inventory from yesterday to today, as much as you differ with your spouse.

REFERENCES

Briggs, K., & Myers, I. (1977). *Myers-Briggs Type Indicator, form G.* Palo Alto, CA: Consulting Psychologists Press.

Briggs-Myers, I., & McCauley, M. (1985). *Manual: A guide to the development and use of the Myers-Briggs Type Indicator.* Palo Alto, CA: Consulting Psychologists Press.

Bruch, M., & Skovholt, T. (1985). Congruence of Holland personality type and marital satisfaction. *Measurement and Evaluation in Counseling and Development, 18*, 100–107.

Burns, R. (1987). *Kinetic-House-Tree-Person drawings: An interpretative manual.* New York: Brunner/Mazel.

Dudek, S. (1954). An approach to fundamental compatibility in marital couples through the Rorschach. *Journal of Projective Techniques, 18*, 400.

Dudek, S., & Gottlieb, S. (1954). An approach to fundamental compatibility in marital couples through the Rorschach. *American Psychologist, 9*, 356.

Haley, J. (1964). Research on family patterns: An instrument measurement. *Family Process, 3*, 41-65.

Hammer, E. (1980). *The clinical application of projective drawings*. Springfield, IL: Charles C Thomas.

Hansen, J. (1984). *User's guide for the SVIB SCII: Strong-Campbell Interest Inventory of the Strong Vocational Interest Blank, form T 325*. Stanford, CA: Stanford University Press.

Harris, D. (1963). *Children's drawings as measures of intellectual maturity*. New York: Harcourt, Brace, and World.

Hathaway, S., & McKinley, J. (1943). *The Minnesota Multiphasic Personality Inventory*. St. Paul, MN: University of Minnesota Press.

Holland, J. (1973). *Making vocational choices: A theory of careers*. Englewood Cliffs, NJ: Prentice-Hall.

Lachar, D. (1977). *The MMPI: Clinical assessment and automated interpretation*. Los Angeles: Western Psychological Services.

Levy, J., & Epstein, N. (1964). An application of the Rorschach test in family investigation. *Family Process, 3*, 344-376.

Loveland, N., Wynne, L., & Singer, M. (1963). The Family Rorschach: A new method for studying family interaction. *Family Process, 2*, 187-215.

Osgood, E., Suci, G., & Tannenbaum, P. (1957). *The measurement of meaning*. Urbana, IL: University of Illinois Press.

Rokeach, M. (1973). *The nature of human values*. New York: The Free Press.

Sarrell, P., Sarrell, L., & Berman, F. (1981). Using the Draw-A-Person (DAP) test in sex therapy. *Journal of Sex and Marital Therapy, 7*, 163-183.

Strong, E., Campbell, D., & Hansen, J. (1985). *Strong-Campbell Interest Inventory of the Strong Vocational Interest Blank, form T 325*. Stanford, CA: Stanford University Press.

Wechsler, D. (1974). *Manual for the Wechsler Intelligence Scale for Children—Revised*. New York: The Psychological Corporation.

Wechsler, D. (1981). *WAIS-R manual: Wechsler Adult Intelligence Scale—Revised*. New York: The Psychological Corporation.

3
Observational Measurements

There is no substitute for direct observation of the family process. Typically, observational measurements give the family a verbal or nonverbal task and then the observer (clinically, the therapist) rates the behaviors. How structured does this observation need to be? Can the interview be refined into a better diagnostic tool? Can a structured series of tasks provide insight to the therapist and her clients so that the pattern of interaction between the spouses might be improved?

What the authors of observational measurements must do is improve on diagnostic techniques that require less training. After all, on some measurements, global impressions are actually superior to precise observations of specific signs (Schmidt & McGowan, 1959). This is especially true when the therapist can think creatively, is able to connect loosely associated ideas, and is socially sensitive to subtle nuances of interpersonal behavior (Handler, 1985).

Authors of observational measurements must overcome the great variation in ability to observe on the part of therapists. Does the client "really" behave the way the therapist reports? Except for clerical errors, paper-and-pencil inventories will produce the same scores regardless of who is marking the paper. Observational measurements, however, produce such different observations by different observers that it often becomes necessary to spend a considerable amount of time training observers to agree with each other.

It is easier to get outside raters to agree about the results of a series of short assignments (e.g., three two-minute problems) than the result of one long assignment (e.g., one six-minute problem). Of course, an assignment can be so short that any global insight is difficult. The amount of time or activity spent must be long enough to cancel out chance unrepresentative behaviors. Something must be done to control the clinician's tendency to play "Spot the pathology." Since the family has usually come with a problem, the diagnostician is under pressure to find something wrong instead of being able to objectively observe. The family does not always cooperate; typically, it is "on best behavior." The diagnostician therefore assumes that any inappropriate behavior is the "truth," even if that behavior is not representative of the entire interview. This assumption is sometimes correct, which is one reason that clinicians and psychometrists speak different languages.

Unfortunately, training observers how to code may not be worth it. Coders seem to code less consistently than otherwise when they believe their consistency is not being checked (Lipinski & Nelson, 1974).

Observational measurements require an immense amount of time to code and to learn how to code. The Marital Interaction Coding System (MICSIII) is perhaps the most widely used marital coding system (Weiss & Summers, 1983). It takes two to three months of weekly instruction and practice to learn how to use its 32 codes. The Couples Interaction Scoring System (CISS) (Notarius & Markman, 1981) initially takes 25–30 minutes to code every minute of observed tape interaction. The CISS, despite its precious acronym, has been used to discover important insights (for example, positive behavior does not come as repayment, but simply to make one's spouse feel good). It has even helped produce a useful paper-and-pencil inventory, which we will describe later (Marital Agendas Protocol). But it is much too long and difficult for actual therapy.

Filsinger (1983) developed a computer-based coding system from MICSIII, CISS, and two other coding systems. If the therapist or therapist trainer is computer-oriented, this coding system—the Dyadic Interaction Scoring Code (DISC)—can save time. A hand-held battery-powered data collector, the Datamyte, is punched by the coder and the data are fed (immediately, if desired) into a computer for analysis. As programs are developed to interpret the data and as computers become more user-friendly, observation scales like DISC will become more appealing.

Finally, the therapist must suggest meaning to observed behaviors. Observation is thought to be superior to self-report because it is superior at measuring behavior. But what do behaviors mean? Can we say behavior X implies attitude Y? Most therapists would say, for example, that eye contact between husband and wife is a good sign of nonverbal communication. Well, most therapists might be wrong. Haynes, Follingstad, and Sullivan (1979) found a higher rate of eye contact between distressed couples than between nondistressed couples. This means, at the very least, that on occasion eye contact is not a dependable sign. Or it might mean that eye contact is simply eye contact. It is positive only if one or both partners regard it as such. Or it might mean that for those people who know each other intimately and who are coming for therapy, eye contact needs to be scored negatively. In summary, we have considerable research to do to enable us to score behaviors.

Partly because different descriptions of marital interaction are given by family members, some effort at observing that interaction seems in order. As a technique, video playback was developed by Alger (1976) and is also discussed in the *Handbook of Structured Techniques in Marriage and Family Therapy* (Sherman & Fredman, 1986). This chapter will present four observational inventories that can be used as therapeutic techniques, but which, with increasing research, show promise of becoming psychometrically sound measurements.

MARITAL AND FAMILY INTERACTION CODING SYSTEM (MFICS)

The Marital and Family Interaction Coding System (MFICS) was developed by Olson and Ryder (1978) to evaluate couple or family performance on the older Inventory of Marital Conflict (IMC) (1970). The inventory consists of two sets of nine case studies each of paragraph length. The case studies involve relationships with families and friends, use of leisure time, jealousy, division of labor, and work/family tensions. In six of the case studies the husband and wife are given slightly different facts. Each spouse individually answers written questions concerning who is responsible for the conflict, what should be done, and the relevance of the case study. This takes about 15 minutes. Then they are asked to discuss the case studies jointly and reach a joint decision concerning responsibility and conflict solution. This takes about 15–30 minutes and is taperecorded. For couples with children, the Inventory of Parent–Child Conflict (IPCC) (Olson & Ryder, 1977) and Inventory of Parent-Adolescent Conflict (IPAC) (Olson, Portner, & Bell, 1977) have been developed.

IMC and its variant forms can be used by the therapist. They provide an objective view of family interaction in relevant life situations that are relatively nonthreatening and enjoyable. The inventories are easy to use and inexpensive. The standardized procedure requires the therapist to be out of the room. If this instruction is followed, the therapist can compare taperecorded with regular therapy session behavior. For the therapist to become familiar with the instrument does require some time.

MFICS generally requires one of 20 codes to evaluate each speech on the IMC. If a speech is longer than a sentence, it may require more than one code. Four areas of interaction have been noted. *Task leadership* notes who initiates discussions, who talks most, who documents opinions, who defers to the other, and who moves the discussion along. *Conflict* notes what aids or hinders joint decisions and on what issue the couple disagrees. For example, are belittling or cutting remarks made? The couple can learn with the therapist's help to identify their own tendencies towards passive, aggressive, or assertive styles. *Affect* notes encouragement and support, similarity of emotional response, criticism, blame, tension, anger, and humor. *Communication Style* notes whether the couple are talking with or at each other, listening, reflecting, or interrupting spontaneously. Sometimes research shows that codes assigned to Communication Style could be assigned to the other three areas.

It takes time to become oriented to both the IMC and MFICS. Once the therapist learns how to code, Olson and Ryder state that it takes 15 to 30 minutes per couple of the therapist's time outside the session to listen to (or watch) the tape and develop interpretations of the couple's behavior. MFICS discovers important aspects of interpersonal problem solving, but its use has been limited to the highly structured set of tasks found on the IMC. Many researchers have used MFICS, and research on the instrument is continuing.

CARD SORT PROCEDURE

Reiss, Oliveri, and associates (Berger, Roe, Oliveri, & Reiss, undated) have developed an observation task procedure that helps identify how the family interprets and interacts with its social environment. Research has demonstrated that the ability to solve the kind of puzzle Reiss and Oliveri present does not relate to the level of education or social status of the participants, yet preadolescent children have difficulty solving the puzzles.

The family members are placed in soundproof booths and are not allowed to discuss the first puzzle with each other. Two decks of 16 cards are placed in each booth. Each card has a row of letters printed on it (for example, A C A Q D T). Each family member is instructed to take the first deck of cards " . . . [which] you are to sort. . . . You may sort the cards into as many columns as you wish, up to and including seven. Seven is the maximum number of columns, although you may use fewer." There are two logical ways to sort the cards: a length solution (sorting according to the number of letters on each card) and a pattern solution (sorting according to the pattern of letters on each card). Reactions of the family to the task (e.g., "This is fun" or "What is this supposed to prove?") are clinically noted, as these reactions are usually consistent with later performance. When each member has finished, a button is pressed, a photograph taken of the results, and the first deck is put out of the way.

When all family members have finished, they remain in their separate booths and are instructed to "pick up the second deck of cards. . . . This puzzle is like the last one . . . [except that] this time you are encouraged to talk about the puzzle among yourselves, if you wish. [And] it is important that you only consider two cards at a time. . . . When you have decided on the best way to sort the first two cards, press your finish button." The results are photographed. Each individual then takes two more cards, has the opportunity to reorder the columns, press the finish button, and again the results are photographed. This continues until all 16 cards have been sorted.

Three dimensions of family problem-solving behavior are measured. *Configuration* measures the degree to which the family average matches the complex solution. The absolute score is secondary. High configuration means that the family scored higher when communication with other family members was possible than when working without such communication. High configuration families are thought to see the world as ordered and understandable, to view themselves as capable of coping, and to be consistent and effective. Low configuration families see the world as baffling and uncontrollable, view themselves as helpless, and are pessimistic and overwhelmed.

The second dimension is *coordination*, which is measured both by the similarity of card sort results and by the similarity of the amount of time taken to complete the sort. High coordination families perceive the family as a group and think the world treats them as a group. Low coordination families perceive the family as a collection of individuals.

The third dimension is *closure*, which is measured by the trial number after which two or more members make no more sorting changes, the average time per trial, and the average number of sorting changes. Those families who delay closure look for the novel in their environment, view the family as evolving, and are open. Those families who make early closure look for the familiar in their environment and view the family as continuing from the past.

Research shows that the three dimensions are independent; that is, families that are high on one dimension may be high, low, or average on the other dimensions. Unfortunately, the Card Sort cannot distinguish between distressed and nondistressed families; it can only describe the fundamental family assumptions about the social environment and the family's place within it—what Oliveri and Reiss (1981) call the "family paradigm." Why families that are thought to see the world as baffling and uncontrollable and themselves as helpless and overwhelmed are no more likely to be distressed than nondistressed is hard to understand. Reiss (1982) and Reiss and Oliveri (1980) urge therapists and researchers to remember the presence or lack of stress and the nature of the rules the family makes to reach its goals. Pathology will not afflict baffled and helpless families until they experience a severe and debilitating crisis and until rules become contradictory and goal-thwarting. However, perhaps the insistence that only the "elegant" pattern answer is correct and the simpler length-of-letter answer is incorrect has confounded the results. The lack of positive findings may be the product of the technique used. Configuration is measured by a change score, and change scores are notoriously subject to errors of measurement.

At present, the Card Sort Procedure is being used at George Washington University to help validate the "family paradigm" theory. In its present form, therapists and researchers can only look at the Procedure from afar. However, a modified Card Sort is reported by Kinston, Loader, and Miller (1985) to be the most popular part of their Family Task Interview (see p. 36). Until the data collecting is simplified we will watch Reiss and Oliveri's continued research to demonstrate the usefulness of the Card Sort Procedure and the power of the "family paradigm" theory.

BEAVERS-TIMBERLAWN FAMILY EVALUATION SCALE

According to dictionary definition (Stein, 1967), "entropy" is "the amount of energy unavailable for work during a natural process. For a system undergoing a spontaneous change, this quantity changes." Beavers (1985) uses the word "negentropy" to mean the precise opposite: energy available for productive work. Fortunately for users of the Beavers-Timberlawn Family Evaluation Scale (BT), the scale itself avoids jargon and is simple to read. In modified form it has served as a model for similar scales (such as the Family Health Scale discussed in this chapter).

Beavers argues that it is more clinically useful to conceptualize a family on a continuum from dysfunctional to functional (or, in biological terms, entropy to negentropy) than to see chaos as one extreme to be avoided, along with its opposite, rigidity. Chaos, he writes, "is actually a very rigid, stereotyped structure, allowing for little change" (Beavers, 1985, p. 3). He compares the history of families to the history of countries that proceed from chaos to dictatorship to moderate dominance to negotiated exchanged leadership to shared leadership.

Families are asked to "discuss as a group what you would like to change about your family." The therapist needs to monitor this exercise, joining in where necessary and watching the family interact. A videotape is made of the last 10 minutes of the session and only the content on this videotape serves as data for the scale. The rater should not use what she imagines might occur elsewhere.

Five basic dimensions are rated. On some dimensions optimum functioning is rated 1; on others, 5. So the user must be aware that simple addition or averaging is not possible without knowing what the numbers mean for each specific scale. A manual explains the theory behind the BT and how to improve rater judgment. The five dimensions are:

I. *Structure of the Family*

   A. *Overt Power*: chaos to absolute control to negotiation to shared leadership

   B. *Parental Coalitions*: parent-child coalition to everyone for himself to strong parental coalition

   C. *Closeness*: vague boundaries to isolation to closeness with distinct boundaries ("In order to be close, you first have to be separate")

II. *Mythology*

   Very congruent to very incongruent (How does the family think it functions versus how it really functions?)

III. *Goal-Directed Negotiation*

   Extremely efficient to extremely inefficient (Do they get job done? How many participate?)

IV. *Autonomy*

   A. *Clarity of Expression*: very clear to hardly anyone clear (disclosing thoughts and feelings)

   B. *Responsibility*: voice responsibility to rarely voice responsibility (family allows mistakes, avoids blame and scapegoating)

   C. *Invasiveness*: many invasions to none (speaking for others, mindreading)

D. *Permeability*: very open to unreceptive (Are people heard regardless of whether they agree?)

V. *Family Affect*

A. *Range of Feelings*: direct expression of a wide range of feelings to little or no expression of feelings (Are feelings allowed?)

B. *Mood and Tone*: warm to polite to hostile to depressed to cynical

C. *Unresolvable Conflict*: severe conflict with severe impairment of family functioning to definite conflict with slight impairment to little or no unreasonable conflict

D. *Empathy*: consistent responsiveness to attempted understanding of others' feelings to grossly inappropriate responses to feelings

A global rating is then made, with 1 as the very best family you have ever had any experience with, to 10 for the very worst. Families rated 10 and 9 are classified severely disturbed, 8 and 7 are borderline, 6 and 5 are midrange, 4 and 3 are adequate, and 2 and 1 are optimal.

Beavers and associates have developed other instruments to enhance the diagnostic process. The Core Assessment Information records ethnicity; religion; number of prior marriages; number of children from previous marriage; name of identified parent(s); the problem; significant physical conditions; medications; type of previous treatment; hypothesis regarding symptom maintenance; support from outside family; time of recent family crisis; triggering event; list of family strengths; therapeutic goals; area of needed intervention; proposed intervention strategy; anticipated length of treatment; specific improvements expected from treatment; and the most likely way the therapist could fail.

From the videotaped session, the Centripetal/Centrifugal Family Style Scale measures on eight subscales and one global scale the degree to which the family has a strong, inner orientation and gratifies itself within the family or within the outside world. Much of this is an expansion of the closeness subscale on the BT.

Finally, a Self-Report Family Inventory (SFI) is available for all family members (12 years of age and older). The SFI is administered to the entire family at the first and last sessions.

The Beavers-Timberlawn Family Evaluation Scale has recently been subject to testing to demonstrate its reliability and usefulness. Variations of the BT have shown that it meets the need of therapists to have a more focused initial interview. Beavers and Voeller (1983) argue that especially in its conception of chaos as extreme rigidity and adaptability as a positive trait, it provides a more clinically useful diagnosis than other instruments.

FAMILY TASK INTERVIEW/FAMILY HEALTH SCALE

Kinston and Loader (1985) are psychiatrists who have treated children with various ailments together with their families at London's Hospital for Sick Children. They are currently creating a structured interview—the Family Task Interview (FTI)—with Miller and others that would be simple, easy to administer, standardized, feel natural, and yet meet reliability and validity standards. Their work is built upon the foundations created by Beavers and Reiss and Oliveri.

The FTI can be used with either one or two parents and one to four children. At least one child has to be over four years of age. Some slight revision is being planned for families with teenagers. The interview takes about 50 minutes plus another five minutes for explanations. Experience has shown that it is necessary to inform the parents of the length of the interview and suggest toilet use, if necessary.

The FTI is conducted in a simply decorated room with a low table and a semicircle of identical chairs. Extra small chairs are provided for young children. A VCR is useful, but not necessary—and, of course, requires family consent. All family members are required to attend.

Kinston, Loader, and associates have found a two-way vision mirror necessary. They suggest an unobtrusive cassette recorder which the family presses to start the interview and then does not touch again. The interview is basically conducted without the therapist present. However, our own students have administered the FTI in family living rooms and were present—off in a corner—while the tasks were performed. There was some mutual embarrassment with disturbed families when the tasks were being performed. Nevertheless, our students were able to avoid family efforts to draw them into the conversation.

The FTI on tape consists of a welcome and a simple presentation of rules. Instructions for each task are repeated twice, and if the family is still unclear, written instructions are available on cards inside envelopes next to the cassette. The family is informed how long they have for each task. At the end of the tape the family is thanked.

Currently, the FTI consists of seven tasks:

Task 1. (four minutes) Plan something together which must take at least an hour.

Task 2. (four minutes) Get the box of blocks and build a tower. A central low table is used. (Note coordination, flexibility, and role shifts).

Task 3. (four minutes) Discuss likes and dislikes of each member. (Note expression of problems, conflicts, wishes for change, and capacity to respect individuality).

Task 4. (nine minutes) Sort a deck of cards in a pattern similar to Reiss's Card Sort Procedure. (Note parent-child interactions, family negotiations, and decision making).

Task 5. (nine minutes) Complete the following story: A family is at home. One member is missing and late returning. The phone rings and the family is asked to come to the hospital urgently.

Task 6. (nine minutes) Parents should choose a well-known saying, decide what it means, then explain it to the children. (Note interaction apart from children and then the process of parenting).

Task 7. (five minutes) Discuss the interview. (Compare the observer's view with the family's view).

The main clinical features of families are revealed. The superiority of the FTI is found most notably in the area of alliances. Typically, alliance patterns are distorted by the way the therapist intrudes into the family system.

The FTI was designed to be innocuous and only a few families rated it uncomfortable. Kinston, Loader, and Miller (1985) report that those tasks requiring activity (the Building Block task and the Card Sorting task) were the best liked. The most disliked tasks were to "complete a (hospital fantasy) story and explain a well-known saying." About two-thirds of the families felt the FTI had revealed typical family behavior, but some felt the procedure was unnatural.

Quantitatively, the FTI is measured by rating the family on the Family Health Scale (FHS). The FHS uses a seven-point scale, rating 1 for a breakdown of family functioning, 3 for clear dysfunction, 5 for adequate functioning, and 7 for optimal functioning. Word descriptions aid the raters in their evaluation. A sample rating scale is illustrated on the next page.

The Family Health Scale takes the clinician 15 to 30 minutes to score and average. Basically, the FHS enables raters to consistently evaluate the Family Task Interview results.

To verify the claim that FTI/FHS is easy to use, we had graduate students in our Marriage and Family classes administer the interview and scale. Although their sole preparation for this task was reading the manual, they were about as consistent as the specifically trained Kinston-Loader group. However, though this was true of the total score, individual subtests required more caution. Videotapes are available at cost to improve scoring reliability.

Kinston, Loader, and Miller (1985) report that studies show that family performance remains stable over time if there has been no therapeutic interference. Families reveal themselves differently on the FTI than they do by self-report. Psychiatrically labeled families score lower on the FTI/FHS than do families with obese, celiac, or regular schoolchildren.

Kinston, Loader, and associates have revised the FTI for clinicians (FTI-C). The FTI is a good example of a family inventory in the process of development from a research instrument to a therapist's tool. It has the advantage over the usual clinical interview of being standardized. Among other things this promises more accuracy on the part of the interviewer, less self-delusion, and growing clinical insight.

The four coding systems discussed in this chapter show promise of moving out of the specific laboratory where they have been developed

Sample Rating Scale for the FHS

Involvement						
Breakdown & Functioning		*Dysfunctional*		*Adequate*		*Optimal*
1	2	3	4	5	6	7
Family members dominate or are withdrawn, actively excluded, or ignored		One or more family members attempts to dominate or has difficulty in participating		Minor degree of inequality of participation		All members able to participate

The areas rated by the FHS are:

1. *Affective Status*:
   Atmosphere, nature of relationship, emotional involvement, affective expression, individual mood

2. *Communication*:
   Continuity, involvement, expression of messages, reception of messages

3. *Boundaries*:
   Relation to environment, cohesion, intergenerational boundary, individual autonomy

4. *Alliances*:
   Pattern of relationships: marital, parental-coalition, parent-child, child-parent, sibling

5. *Adaptability and Stability*:
   Stability, adaptability to environment, family organization flexibility

6. *Family Competence*:
   Conflict resolution, decision making, problem solving, parental management of children

into family therapist training centers and slowly (especially with the increased use of the VCR) into clinical use. Reiss and Oliveri's Card Sort Procedure has a rich theoretical base and increasing research behind it. In its original form it is too laboratory-centered for clinical use. But, as we have noted, Kinston and Loader's Family Task Interview has used a modified Card Sort Procedure – unfortunately, without the theoretical interpretations of Reiss and Oliveri. Kinston and Loader's Family Health Scale can be utilized by the practicing therapist. Like Olson and Ryder's Marital and Family Interaction Coding System, the Family Health Scale is adapted to a particular set of tasks: MFICS to standardized verbal tasks and FHS to sometimes verbal, sometimes nonverbal tasks. FHS owes much to the Beavers-Timberlawn Family Evaluation Scale. This latter scale has one advantage over the other instruments discussed: the specific task is already used by many therapists. The family is asked, "Discuss, as a group, what you would like to change about your family."

Kinston and Loader's Family Health Scale and the Beavers-Timberlawn Family Evaluation Scale both use a more global way of reporting, with no significant loss in rater agreement. The amount of time required for all four observation systems becomes reasonable once the coding system is learned. The meaning of the behaviors seems most apparent in Beaver's scale, but considerable research on all four instruments enhances not only the specific observation inventories but also our understanding of structured interaction.

REFERENCES

Alger, I. (1976). Integrating immediate video playback in family therapy. In P. Guerin (Ed.), *Family therapy: Theory and practice*. New York: Gardner Press.

Beavers, R. (1985). *Manual of Beavers-Timberlawn Family Evaluation Scale and Family Style Evaluation*. Dallas: Southwest Family Institute.

Beavers, R., & Voeller, M. (1983). Family models: Comparing and contrasting the Olson Circumplex Model with the Beavers System Model. *Family Process, 22*, 85–98.

Berger, K., Roe, P., Oliveri, M., & Reiss, D. (undated). *Manual of Card Sort Procedure*. Washington: Center for Family Research, George Washington University School of Medicine.

Filsinger, E. (1983). A machine-aided marital observation technique. The

Dyadic Interaction Scoring Code. *Journal of Marriage and the Family, 45*, 623-632.

Handler, L. (1985). The clinical use of the Draw-A-Person Test (DAP). In C. Newmark (Ed.), *Major psychological assessment instruments*. Boston: Allyn and Bacon.

Haynes, S., Follingstad, T., & Sullivan, J. (1979). Assessment of marital satisfaction and interaction. *Journal of Consulting and Clinical Psychology, 47*, 789-791.

Kinston, W., Loader, P., & Miller, L. (1985). *Clinical assessment of family health*. London: Hospital for Sick Children, Family Studies Group.

Lipinski, D., & Nelson, R. (1974). Problems in the use of naturalistic observation as a means of behavior assessment. *Behavioral Therapy, 5*, 341-351.

Notarius, C., & Markman, H. (1981). Couples Interaction Scoring System. In E. Filsinger & R. Lewis (Eds.), *Assessing marriage: New behavioral approaches*. Beverly Hills, CA: Sage.

Oliveri, M., & Reiss, D. (1981). A theory-based empirical classification of family problem behavior. *Family Process, 20*, 409-418.

Olson, D., & Ryder, R. (1970). Inventory of Marital Conflict (IMC). An experimental interaction procedure. *Journal of Marriage and the Family, 32(3)*, 443-448.

Olson, D., & Ryder, R. (1977). *Inventory of Parent-Child Conflict*. St. Paul: Family Social Science, University of Minnesota.

Olson, D., Portner, J., & Bell, R. (1977). *Inventory of Parent-Adolescent Conflict*. St. Paul: Family Social Science, University of Minnesota.

Olson, D., & Ryder, R. (1978). *Marital and Family Interaction Coding System (MFICS): Abbreviated coding manual*. St. Paul: Family Social Science, University of Minnesota.

Reiss, D. (1982). The working family: A researcher's view of health in the household. *American Journal of Psychiatry, 139*, 1412-1420.

Reiss, D., & Oliveri, M. (1980). Family paradigm and family coping: A proposal for linking the family's intrinsic adaptive capacities to its responses to stress. *Family Relations, 29*, 431-444.

Schmidt, L., & McGowan, J. (1959). The differentiation of human figure drawing. *Journal of Consulting Psychology, 23*, 129-133.

Sherman, R., & Fredman, N. (1986). *Handbook of structured techniques in marriage and family therapy*. New York: Brunner/Mazel.

Stein, J. (Ed.). (1967). *The Random House Dictionary of the English Language*. New York: Random House.

Weiss, R., & Summers, K. (1983). Marital Interaction Coding System III. In E. Filsinger (Ed.), *Marriage and family assessment: A sourcebook of family therapy*. Beverly Hills, CA: Sage.

4

General Marital Satisfaction and Adjustment Scales

INTRODUCTION

The "granddaddy" of marriage scales was written by Terman (1938), "Mr. Stanford" of the Stanford-Binet. It was much too long. And Terman begat Locke-Wallace. Since most modern family questionnaires "prove" their validity by comparing their results with the Locke-Wallace, examination of this instrument (the earliest in our collection) makes an informative beginning. Hunt (1978) suggested that the Locke-Wallace Marital Adjustment Test (see Measure #1) could still be used if practitioners and researchers simplified the scoring: "On a scale of 0 for unhappy to 6 for perfectly happy, how do you rate your marriage?"

Twenty years passed, 30 since Locke's early publications. And Locke-Wallace begat Spanier. Spanier's Dyadic Adjustment Scale (see Measure #2) drops the 35 questions Locke-Wallace used to predict marital success. Who really dared to say to a client, "You are too grouchy and too poorly educated to get married"? Spanier expanded and updated those parts of the Locke-Wallace that measured consensus, cohesion, and affectional expression. Except for affectional expression, the subscales are quite reliable.

Roach, Frazier, and Bowden have constructed the Marital Satisfaction Scale (see Measure #3) that measures a single factor, marital satisfaction. Why construct a 48-item scale to measure only one thing? Research using this scale shows that it is reliable, sensitive to change in the marital relationship, and, unlike Locke-Wallace, does not phrase questions in a way that stimulates unrealistic, this-is-a-perfect-relationship-type responses.

Snyder's Marital Satisfaction Inventory (MSI) (see Measure #4) is commercially published by Western Psychological Services. Its title earns it placement in this chapter as do subscales of "disharmony" (18 items) for the general population and "disaffection" (26 items) for couples in therapy. Actually the MSI can be used for more than general marital satisfaction. There are 11 scales measuring such specifics as childrearing conflict, sexual dissatisfaction, and unhappy childhood as well as the more global measures of general satisfaction.

Notarius and Vanzetti produced the Marital Agendas Protocol (see Measure #5), an index that actually leaves blank spaces for the clinician or researcher to add problem areas, or "agendas." It takes less time than most general satisfaction inventories (five minutes), and asks each spouse to consider 10 common issues "all marriages must face." Like the commonly used "problem checklists," it is a communication to the therapist and indirectly to the spouse that the client wants to talk. The uniqueness of the protocol is question 2: the expectancy each partner has that the problems can be resolved.

Two important theorists in family therapy are McMaster and Moos. McMaster's Model of Family Functioning has inspired a 53-item questionnaire by Epstein and his colleagues: the McMaster Family Assessment Device (FAD) (see Measure #6). Six areas of family functioning are evaluated. Considerable work continues to be done with the instrument. At the very least, the instrument contains a highly reliable, yet brief (12-item) measure of general functioning.

"Marriage is an institution" is more than the first line of a tired joke; it is a way of conceptualizing marital relations. Rudolph Moos and his colleagues developed a series of scales to evaluate the way institutions maintain or change themselves and provide opportunities for relationships and personal development. He has already developed instruments to measure such institutions as schools, the military, prisons, jobs, and therapeutic groups. Now he and Bernice Moos produced the Family Environment Scale (FES) (see Measure #7). The 90-item 10-subscale instrument measures relationship, personal growth, and system maintenance dimensions.

Udry's Marital Alternatives Scale (see Measure #8) measures the other side of marital satisfaction: Could a spouse do any better by not being married (at least to this partner)? This chilling scale adds information that cannot be found in a marital satisfaction survey. It is a better prediction of divorce and separation than the marital satisfaction scales. We are required to ask ourselves if measuring the attitude towards separation and divorce increases that likelihood.

Lowman's Inventory of Family Feelings (see Measure #9) measures one—and only one—dimension of interpersonal relationship: the strength of positive feeling. A neutral response is treated as a nonpositive feeling. Each family member completes the 38-item inventory that measures his attitudes towards all the individuals in the family. What is revealed quite well are positive and scapegoating coalitions and the ability to give and receive affection. This inventory can also measure relationships with parents and in-laws.

REFERENCES

Hunt, R. (1978). The effect of item weighting on the Locke-Wallace Marital Adjustment Scale. *Journal of Marriage and the Family, 40,* 249–256.

Terman, L. (1938). *Psychological factors in marital happiness.* New York: McGraw-Hill.

1 | MARITAL ADJUSTMENT TEST

Harvey Locke and Karl Wallace

Introduction

Even in the 1980s authors try to prove the validity of their marriage adjustment inventories by correlating their results with the Locke-Wallace. So, if only to keep it honest, it is necessary to examine the 15-item Marital Adjustment Test that the other scales use as the standard.

Description

Marital adjustment scales had existed for years before Locke-Wallace, but they were very long. The two parts of Terman's inventory (1938) (for adjustment and for prediction), for example, had 257 items; the two parts of Burgess-Wallin Marital Success Schedule (1953), 379. Even researchers would not use such lengthy inventories. Locke and Wallace felt that by choosing the items that are the most basic and which had the greatest correlation with the total test score they could construct a short, reliable, and valid inventory. They produced a 15-item Marital Adjustment Test and a 35-item Marital Prediction Test. The Marital Prediction Test is no longer used by researchers or clinicians.

The Marital Adjustment Test contains one global adjustment question, eight questions measuring areas of possible disagreement, and six questions measuring conflict resolution, cohesion, and communication.

Each response to each item has a different weight. These point values were chosen according to the amount of difference discovered between groups of satisfied and problem couples answering each alternative. Total adjustment scores range from 2 to 158 points.

Sample

The sample consisted of 118 husbands and 118 wives *not* married to each other. The men averaged about 29 years; the women averaged about 30. Fifteen percent of the subjects' fathers were born in northern

Europe, 81% were whites born in the United States. The mean education level was 15 years for men, 14 for women. Seventy-three percent were Protestant, 11% Catholic, 5% Jewish, 11% without religious affiliation. Fifty-four percent of the men were professionals, salesmen, or semiprofessionals; 58% of the women were housewives and the majority of the remainder secretaries, clerks, skilled or semiskilled workers. Forty percent of the men had no children, 39% one child; 48% of the women had no children, 27% one child. No one was married less than one year; on the average the members of the sample had been married for five-and-a-half years.

For the validity study 22 men and 26 women who were divorced, separated, or seeking marital therapy were matched for age and sex, with 48 persons in the sample "judged to be exceptionally well adjusted in marriage by friends who knew them well."

Reliability

The internal consistency reliability estimate for the 15-item adjustment test was a high .90. No test–retest reliabilities are reported.

Validity

The adjustment test discriminated significantly between the adjusted and maladjusted groups. Only 17% of the maladjusted group scored 100 or more; 96% of the adjusted group scored 100 or more. Unfortunately, the Locke-Wallace correlates very highly (.63) with a conventionalization scale, meaning that it tends to bring out the desire of people to describe their marriage as happier and better than it really is.

Administration

The Locke-Wallace is a 15-item, paper-and-pencil inventory that takes two to 10 minutes. It is graded by the therapist. Grading by Hunt's simplified system is as follows:

- item 1: score 0-6
- items 2-9: score 0-5

- items 10, 14: score 0-2
- items 11, 13: score 0-3
- item 12: disagree score 0
  agree "on the go" score 1
  agree "at home" score 2
- item 15: score 0,1,2,2
- Maximum score = 60

Location

Locke, H., & Wallace K. (1959). Short marital adjustment and prediction tests: Their reliability and validity. *Marriage and Family Living, 2*, 251-255.

Discussion

Why is the 15-item Marital Adjustment Test not being used by more than test researchers? A reliability of .90 is impressive. Primarily, therapists would prefer a test where each item received 0 or 1 point, or 0 to 5 points. Two for this and 15 for that could lead not only to arguments but to arithmetic errors as well. But there is some good news: Hunt (1978) demonstrated that an unweighted Locke-Wallace in which items would receive 0 to 5 points for six possible responses would produce the same results as the weighted original (r = .92 for wives, .94 for husbands).

Some of the items are out of date. Fifty-eight percent of the women in the sample were housewives and the majority of the remainder were in stereotypically women's jobs. Would a couple in 1987 be less adjusted if they *both* wanted to spend their leisure time "on the go" rather than spend their time at home?

The items of the Locke-Wallace are still a good view of the research on marriage stability. Indeed, 11 of the items are used by Spanier's "new" Dyadic Adjustment Scale (see Measure #2). Students of marriage therapy might spend some time looking at the items and even the various points originally given to each response.

REFERENCES

Burgess, E., & Wallin, P. (1953). *Engagement and marriage*. Philadelphia: J. B. Lippincott.

Hunt, R. A. (1978). The effect of item weighting on the Locke-Wallace Marital Adjustment Scale. *Journal of Marriage and the Family, 40*, 249–256.

Terman, L. (1938). *Psychological factors in marital happiness*. New York: McGraw-Hill.

Marital Adjustment Test

1. Check the dot on the scale line below which best describes the degree of happiness, everything considered, of your present marriage. The middle point, "happy," represents the degree of happiness which most people get from marriage, and the scale gradually ranges on one side to those few who are very unhappy in marriage, and on the other, to those few who experience extreme joy or felicity in marriage.

• • • • • • •

Very Unhappy	Happy	Perfectly Happy

State the approximate extent of agreement or disagreement between you and your mate on the following items. Please check each column.

	Always Agree	Almost Always Agree	Occasionally Disagree	Frequently Disagree	Almost Always Disagree	Always Disagree
2. Handling family finances						
3. Matters of recreation						
4. Demonstrations of affection						
5. Friends						
6. Sex relations						
7. Conventionality (right, good, or proper conduct)						
8. Philosophy of life						
9. Ways of dealing with in-laws						

(continued)

Please underline the one response that you feel best describes your marriage.

10. When disagreements arise, they usually result in:
    husband giving in
    wife giving in
    agreement by mutual give and take
11. Do you and your mate engage in outside interests together?
    all of them
    some of them
    very few of them
    none of them
12. In leisure time do you generally prefer:
    to be "on the go"
    to stay at home
    Does your mate generally prefer:
    to be "on the go"
    to stay at home
13. Do you ever wish you had not married?
    frequently
    occasionally
    rarely
    never
14. If you had your life to live over, do you think you would:
    marry the same person
    marry a different person
    not marry at all
15. Do you confide in your mate:
    almost never
    rarely
    in most things
    in everything

---

2 | DYADIC ADJUSTMENT SCALE

Graham B. Spanier

Introduction

The Dyadic Adjustment Scale was designed as an assessment tool for measuring the quality of adjustment in marriage and other dyads. This 32-item scale has four subscales and can be used with either married or unmarried couples who are living together in a marital-type relationship.

Description

The Dyadic Adjustment Scale is a paper-and-pencil test, two pages in length, which can be self-administered. The test can also be adapted for use in an interview setting. The test includes four subscales which measure dyadic satisfaction, dyadic cohesion, dyadic consensus, and affectional expression.

The scale is designed to serve a number of different needs. First, it can be used as an overall measure of the couple's adjustment. Second, it allows researchers with more limited needs to use one or more of the subscales alone without losing much confidence in the reliability or validity of the instrument.

Of the 32 scale items, 13 measure dyadic consensus, 10 measure dyadic satisfaction, five measure dyadic cohesion, and four measure affectional expression.

The source of the items included in the scale varies. Some items were selected from other scales and others were developed specifically for the scale. Briefly, the process used for item selection was as follows:

1. All items which could be located in any marital adjustment or related scale were identified. This produced approximately 300 items.
2. All duplicate items were then eliminated.
3. Three judges, other than the author, then examined all remaining items. To be acceptable, an item had to be judged relevant for

relationships in the 1970s and had to be an indicator of marital adjustment or a closely related concept.

4. The 200 remaining items were modified where necessary to make them more complete and 25 new items were tried.
5. Statistical tests were then used to eliminate unacceptable items, the 32 that remained comprise the present scale. These items significantly discriminated between divorced and married couples and could be grouped to make important subscales.

A person taking this test can obtain a score from 0 to 151. The higher the score, the better is the person's adjustment to the marriage.

The instructions of the test are clear and concise: "Most persons have disagreements in their relationships. Please indicate below the approximate extent of agreement or disagreement between you and your partner for each item on the following list."

Sample

The questionnaire was given to 218 white married people in central Pennsylvania. The sample consisted primarily of working- and middle-class residents who worked for one of four industrial or corporate firms which agreed to take part in the study.

Questionnaires were also mailed to every person in Centre County, Pennsylvania, who had obtained a divorce during the past year. These people were located through the county divorce records. This group was directed to respond to the questions on the basis of the last month they spent with their former spouses. Ninety-four usable questionnaires were obtained from the sample of approximately 400 located.

A small sample of never-married cohabiting couples were also given the questionnaire.

No significant differences were found between male and female scores.

Reliability

Reliability for the entire 32-item scale is quite high (.96) and surprisingly high for the subscales: Dyadic Consensus (.90), Dyadic Satisfaction (.94), and Dyadic Cohesion (.86). Only the four-item Affectional

Expression subscale has a reliability that dictates considerable caution (.73).

Validity

Items involved in the scale were evaluated by three judges for content validity. Items were included if they met the following criteria:

1. They had to be considered relevant measures of dyadic adjustment for contemporary relationships in the 1970s.
2. They had to be consistent with definitions previously suggested by Spanier and Cole (1974) for adjustment and the components of satisfaction, cohesion, and consensus.
3. They had to be carefully worded with appropriate responses.

The married sample had significantly higher scores than did the divorced sample (114.8 versus 70.7).

The Locke-Wallace Marital Adjustment Test, a frequently used scale for measuring marital adjustment, was selected to assess how the Dyadic Adjustment Scale correlated with other similar scales. The correlation between the scales was .86 among married respondents and .88 among divorced respondents.

Administration

This scale is a short paper-and-pencil inventory, which can be self-administered in just a few minutes. The clients should fill out the form separately and not discuss their answers with each other before completing the scale.

Location

Spanier, G. (1976). Measuring dyadic adjustment: New scales for assessing the quality of marriage and similar dyads. *Journal of Marriage and the Family, 38*, 15–28.

Spanier, G. B., & Filsinger, E. (1983). The Dyadic Adjustment Scale. In E. Filsinger (Ed.), *Marriage and family assessment*. Beverly Hills: Sage.

Discussion

The Dyadic Adjustment Scale appears to be a reliable, valid, and relevant measure which can be used in research on marital and nonmarital dyadic relationships. Although a brief, very simple scale, this instrument appears to yield quite a bit of information.

The average score reported for divorced couples may be too low since the items were chosen in large part for their specific ability to discriminate between a specific sample of married and divorced couples. No retesting was done to find if these items would produce similar results in another group of married and divorced couples.

The low reliability for the Affectional Expression subscale means that care must be taken in interpreting this subscale.

No longitudinal studies are available to determine if the test can predict divorce. No data are available on how the scales pinpoint problems and help diagnose which specific aspects of the relationship are causing the problems.

The Dyadic Adjustment Scale might prove useful in discussing relationships with clients. Its phenomenally high correlation with the Locke-Wallace means that, in effect, it is an alternate form of that classic test.

REFERENCE

Spanier, G., & Cole, C. (1974). Toward clarification and investigation of marital adjustment. *International Journal of Sociology of the Family, 6*, 121-146.

Dyadic Adjustment Scale

		Always agree	Almost always agree	Occasionally disagree	Frequently disagree	Almost always disagree	Always disagree
Cn	1. Handling family finances	5	4	3	2	1	0
Cn	2. Matters of recreation	5	4	3	2	1	0
Cn	3. Religious matters	5	4	3	2	1	0
A	4. Demonstrations of affection	5	4	3	2	1	0
Cn	5. Friends	5	4	3	2	1	0
A	6. Sex relations	5	4	3	2	1	0
Cn	7. Conventionality (correct or proper behavior)	5	4	3	2	1	0
Cn	8. Philosophy of life	5	4	3	2	1	0
Cn	9. Ways of dealing with parents or in-laws	5	4	3	2	1	0
Cn	10. Aims, goals, and things believed important	5	4	3	2	1	0
Cn	11. Amount of time spent together	5	4	3	2	1	0
Cn	12. Making major decisions	5	4	3	2	1	0
Cn	13. Household tasks	5	4	3	2	1	0
Cn	14. Leisure-time interests and activities	5	4	3	2	1	0
Cn	15. Career decisions	5	4	3	2	1	0

		All the time	Most of the time	More often than not	Occasionally	Rarely	Never
S	16. How often do you discuss or have you considered divorce, separation, or terminating your relationship?	0	1	2	3	4	5
S	17. How often do you or your mate leave the house after a fight?	0	1	2	3	4	5
S	18. In general, how often do you think that things between you and your partner are going well?	5	4	3	2	1	0
S	19. Do you confide in your mate?	5	4	3	2	1	0
S	20. Do you ever regret that you married (or lived together)?	0	1	2	3	4	5
S	21. How often do you and your partner quarrel?	0	1	2	3	4	5
S	22. How often do you and your mate "get on each other's nerves"?	0	1	2	3	4	5
		Every day		Almost every day	Occasionally	Rarely	Never
S	23. Do you kiss your mate?	4		3	2	1	0
		All of them		Most of them	Some of them	Very few of them	None of them
C	24. Do you and your mate engage in outside interests together?	4		3	2	1	0
	How often would you say the following occur between you and your mate:						

(continued)

A = Affectional Expression; C = Dyadic Cohesion; Cn = Dyadic Consensus; S = Dyadic Satisfaction.

Dyadic Adjustment Scale (*continued*)

			Never	Less than once a month	Once or twice a month	Once or twice a week	Once a day	More often
C	25.	Have a stimulating exchange of ideas	0	1	2	3	4	5
C	26.	Laugh together	0	1	2	3	4	5
C	27.	Calmly discuss something	0	1	2	3	4	5
C	28.	Work together on a project	0	1	2	3	4	5

These are some things about which couples agree and sometimes disagree. Indicate if either item below caused differences of opinions or were problems in your relationship during the past few weeks. (Check yes or no.)

		Yes	No	
A	29.	0	1	Being too tired for sex
A	30.	0	1	Not showing love

S 31. The dots on the following line represent different degrees of happiness in your relationship. The point, "happy," represents the degree of happiness of most relationships. Please circle the dot that best describes the degree of happiness, all things considered, of your relationship.

0	1	2	3	4	5	6
•	•	•	•	•	•	•
Extremely *un*happy	Fairly *un*happy	A little *un*happy	Happy	Very happy	Extremely happy	Perfect

S 32. Which of the following statements best describes how you feel about the future of your relationship:

5 I want desperately for my relationship to succeed and would go to almost any lengths to see that it does.
4 I want very much for my relationship to succeed and will do all that I can to see that it does.
3 I want very much for my relationship to succeed and will do my fair share to see that it does.
2 It would be nice if my relationship succeeded, and I can't do much more than I am doing now to help it succeed.
1 It would be nice if it succeeded, but I refuse to do any more than I am doing now to keep the relationship going.
0 My relationship can never succeed, and there is no more that I can do to keep the relationship going.

A = Affectional Expression; C = Dyadic Cohesion; S = Dyadic Satisfaction

3 | MARITAL SATISFACTION SCALE: FORM B

Arthur J. Roach, Larry P. Frazier, and Sharon R. Bowden

Introduction

The Marital Satisfaction Scale (MSS): Form B was designed to measure the effectiveness of counseling intervention. The scale is an attitudinal survey with an easy scoring system using 48 items selected to measure general marital satisfaction without eliciting the tendency of survey takers to distort their responses in order to look good.

Description

The MSS is a 48-item, paper-and-pencil questionnaire that uses a single answering format. Response categories are "strongly agree," "agree," "neutral (undecided)," "disagree," "strongly disagree." Half the items are phrased unfavorably towards marriage; half the items are phrased favorably. Scoring for each item ranges from 1 to 5, with 5 indicating the most favorable attitude.

Items were chosen to emphasize opinion rather than recall of facts. Each item is capable of change in a retest situation. Each item evokes a range of agreement or disagreement in a normal population and tends to elicit extreme favorability or unfavorability rather than the more neutral responses. Items that attribute perfection to a spouse or relationship were avoided.

From a 73-item scale, 48 items were chosen for their ability to produce a meaningful (single factor), reliable score that was sensitive to change in the marital relationship.

Sample

The pilot study used 88 subjects, most of whom were Texas school counselors. About half were black, two-thirds were female, and 44% were in their thirties. Eighty percent of the scores indicated satisfaction with marriage.

A second study added 221 subjects. Now the total sample was 55%

female, 19% black, 8% Mexican-American, college-educated, typically graduate students in their twenties from Texas. No differences between men's and women's scores were found.

A third study involved 30 married couples in therapy or selected by peers. Half were categorized as satisfied with marriage; half were not satisfied. The sample was predominantly 20 to 39 years of age, white, college educated, and middle-class Texans, a large percentage of whom were education majors.

The 369 subjects thus represented whites, blacks, and Hispanics. They were unique in being predominantly college-educated, middle-class Texans, a large percentage of whom were education majors.

Reliability

The internal consistency estimate of the MSS is very high, .97, high enough to risk developing a shorter Scale, Form B, with 20 items.

Test–retest reliability for at least three weeks was a respectable .76. The subjects used to determine test–retest reliability, however, were individuals who had requested feedback about their original scores.

Validity

Although the MSS correlated a very high .79 with the Locke-Wallace Marital Adjustment Test, it correlated insignificantly with two measures of social desirability. The test significantly distinguished between couples rated by counselors and peers as satisfied or dissatisfied with their marriages. A sex therapy workshop reported significant changes in scores between pretest and posttest. A later posttest given three weeks after the workshop showed that the improvement scores had been maintained.

Administration

The MSS is a 48-item, paper-and-pencil test which can be self-administered and easily graded.

Location

Roach, A. J., Frazier, L. P., & Bowden, S. R. (1981). The Marital Satisfaction Scale: Development of a measure for intervention research. *Journal of Marriage and the Family, 41*, 537-545.

Discussion

The MSS has been demonstrated to measure the important dimension of satisfaction with considerable reliability. One is tempted to wonder how representative is a sample of 369 volunteer middle-class Texan graduate students. Additional studies with other populations are being conducted.

The scale has shown some ability in avoiding items that tempt unreasonable descriptions of the relationship as perfect. This does not mean, of course, that faking is not easy.

The MSS has been used effectively to measure the success of a marriage workshop and it is for such a purpose and for research that the scale could be recommended.

Marital Satisfaction Scale: Form B

Item	Strongly Agree	Agree	Neutral (undecided)	Disagree	Strongly Disagree
1. I know what my spouse expects of me in our marriage.	SA	A	N	D	SD
2. My spouse could make things easier for me if he/she cared to.	SA	A	N	D	SD
3. I worry a lot about my marriage.	SA	A	N	D	SD
4. If I could start over again, I would marry someone other than my present spouse.	SA	A	N	D	SD
5. I can always trust my spouse.	SA	A	N	D	SD
6. My life would seem empty without my marriage.	SA	A	N	D	SD
7. My marriage is too confining to suit me.	SA	A	N	D	SD
8. I feel that I am "in a rut" in my marriage.	SA	A	N	D	SD
9. I know where I stand with my spouse.	SA	A	N	D	SD
10. My marriage has a bad effect on my health.	SA	A	N	D	SD
11. I become upset, angry, or irritable because of things that occur in my marriage.	SA	A	N	D	SD
12. I feel competent and fully able to handle my marriage.	SA	A	N	D	SD
13. My present marriage is not one I would wish to remain in permanently.	SA	A	N	D	SD

14. I expect my marriage to give me increasing satisfaction the longer it continues.	SA	A	N	D	SD
15. I get discouraged trying to make my marriage work out.	SA	A	N	D	SD
16. I consider my marital situation to be as pleasant as it should be.	SA	A	N	D	SD
17. My marriage gives me more real personal satisfaction than anything else I do.	SA	A	N	D	SD
18. I think my marriage gets more difficult for me each year.	SA	A	N	D	SD
19. My spouse gets me badly flustered and jittery.	SA	A	N	D	SD
20. My spouse gives me sufficient opportunity to express my opinions.	SA	A	N	D	SD
21. I have made a success of my marriage so far.	SA	A	N	D	SD
22. My spouse regards me as an equal.	SA	A	N	D	SD
23. I must look outside my marriage for those things that make life worthwhile and interesting.	SA	A	N	D	SD
24. My spouse inspires me to do my best work.	SA	A	N	D	SD
25. My marriage has "smothered" my personality.	SA	A	N	D	SD
26. The future of my marriage looks promising to me.	SA	A	N	D	SD
27. I am really interested in my spouse.	SA	A	N	D	SD
28. I get along well with my spouse.	SA	A	N	D	SD
29. I am afraid of losing my spouse through divorce.	SA	A	N	D	SD
30. My spouse makes unfair demands on my free time.	SA	A	N	D	SD
31. My spouse seems unreasonable in his/her dealings with me.	SA	A	N	D	SD
32. My marriage helps me toward the goals I have set for myself.	SA	A	N	D	SD

(*continued*)

Marital Satisfaction Scale: Form B *(continued)*

Item	Strongly Agree	Agree	Neutral (undecided)	Disagree	Strongly Disagree
33. My spouse is willing to make helpful improvements in our relationships.	SA	A	N	D	SD
34. My marriage suffers from disagreement concerning matters of recreation.	SA	A	N	D	SD
35. Demonstrations of affection by me and my spouse are mutually acceptable.	SA	A	N	D	SD
36. An unhappy sexual relationship is a drawback in my marriage.	SA	A	N	D	SD
37. My spouse and I agree on what is right and proper conduct.	SA	A	N	D	SD
38. My spouse and I do not share the same philosophy of life.	SA	A	N	D	SD
39. My spouse and I enjoy several mutually satisfying outside interests together.	SA	A	N	D	SD
40. I sometimes wish I had not married my present spouse.	SA	A	N	D	SD
41. My present marriage is definitely unhappy.	SA	A	N	D	SD
42. I look forward to sexual activity with my spouse with pleasant anticipation.	SA	A	N	D	SD
43. My spouse lacks respect for me.	SA	A	N	D	SD
44. I have definite difficulty confiding in my spouse.	SA	A	N	D	SD
45. Most of the time my spouse understands the way I feel.	SA	A	N	D	SD
46. My spouse does not listen to what I have to say.	SA	A	N	D	SD
47. I frequently enjoy pleasant conversations with my spouse.	SA	A	N	D	SD
48. I am definitely satisfied with my marriage.	SA	A	N	D	SD

4 | MARITAL SATISFACTION INVENTORY

Douglas K. Snyder

Introduction

The Marital Satisfaction Inventory (MSI) is a 280-item, true–false questionnaire whose profile resembles the Minnesota Multiphasic Personality Inventory (MMPI). This well-known personality inventory had been constructed by asking questions of mental hospital patients and visitors and choosing items that elicited responses that could distinguish between the patients and the visitors. These produced 10 scales that measured 10 possible pathologies. Then scales were devised that measured the test taker's tendencies to make an extremely good impression (or lie), to make a moderately good impression, or to make a terrible impression.

The scales of the MSI of course do not represent possible pathologies but rather possible sources of marital dissatisfaction. In addition, the items were not chosen by their proven ability to distinguish between typical families and families receiving therapy. The MSI is a 280-item, true-false inventory that has one scale to measure the tendency to make a good impression about the marriage, one global satisfaction scale, three scales that measure the general quality of communication and time together, five scales that measure specific sources of marital distress, and one scale to measure the stress and ineffective role models found in the client's original families.

Description

Originally 440 true–false items were collected from the literature and divided into 11 nonoverlapping scales. A pilot study reduced the scale to 280 items selected for their correlation with the total score. The last 41 items relate to children and childrearing and are placed at the end of the MSI so that they do not need to be answered by childless couples. The 11 scales and the number of items in each scale are:

- Conventionalization (21): the tendency to exaggerate the success of the marriage;

- Global Distress (43): the overall dissatisfaction with the marriage;
- Affective Communication (26): complaints about lack of affection, understanding, and self disclosure;
- Problem Solving Communication (38): tendency for problems to become major and unresolved;
- Time Together (20): lack of time together and common interests;
- Disagreement about Finances (22);
- Sexual Dissatisfaction (25);
- Role Orientation (25): rejection of women's homemaker role;
- Family History of Distress (15): unhappy parental marriage, unhappy childhood, and unhappy relations;
- Dissatisfaction with Children (22); and
- Conflict over Childrearing (19).

Snyder then added two new scales: Disaffection, which selected 26 items using factor analysis on the 127 items dealing with affection; and Disharmony, which selected 18 items that reflect the inability to resolve conflicts. For the general population the Disharmony scale identifies couples in trouble; for couples in therapy the Disaffection scale is more useful.

Sample

The pilot study used 42 couples from the general population and 13 couples in therapy. To select items, the study used 111 couples from an urban community in the southeastern United States selected by a random sampling procedure and 30 couples in therapy. To establish norms most of the responses of the 111 couples were used plus responses of other husbands and wives from a large midwestern city to enable the sample to resemble an appropriately representative sample of Americans (at least midwest and southeastern Americans). The norm sample had 322 husbands (average age 36) and 328 wives (average age 34) who had been married an average of $11^{1}/_{2}$ years. Seventy-seven percent were white, 22% black.

Forty-seven percent were Protestant, 27% Catholic, 4% Jewish, 10% other, and 12% had no religious affiliation.

Forty percent had a BA or better; 37% had some education beyond high school; 23% had only a high school diploma.

Forty-two percent were professionals, administrators, and managers; 18% were clerks and technicians; 16% were semiskilled or skilled laborers; 24% were unskilled or unemployed. No report is given of what percentage were full-time housewives. Did MSI include them among the managers or the unemployed? The first description is economically misleading; the second description is absurd.

Reliability

The internal consistency reliability estimates for all scales were high: from .80 for Dissatisfaction to .97 for Global Distress. The average coefficient was .88. These estimates might be a bit high since they combined the results of the general population with a large sample of results of people in marital therapy.

Stability estimates of the scores over six weeks were very high: from .84 for Affective Communication to .94 for Family History of Distress. The average correlation was .89. Interestingly but not surprisingly, no persons in therapy were used to measure stability of scores.

Validity

Factor analysis was not used to discover if indeed there were 11 areas. Instead, the 11 scale scores were used to discover four factors: a general versus specific feeling factor; a factor that measures child-related skills; a factor that measures conflict between parents and children both in the family of origin and current family; and a factor that measures the traditional versus nontraditional view of women's role.

All 11 scales significantly discriminated between couples in marital therapy and nondistressed couples from the general population. Physically abused women with lower MSI profiles were more likely to return to their husbands than physically abused women with higher scores.

Comparison between clinician interview ratings of the couple and relevant scale scores produced low but statistically meaningful correlations. Parents of psychiatrically hospitalized children had significantly higher scores on Dissatisfaction with Children.

Administration

The MSI is a commercially produced 280-item, true-false self-report intended for couples married or living together for at least six months. It may be appropriate for engaged couples. The last 41 items are devoted to conflicts with children and childrearing and the test booklet indicates that childless couples should not answer these items.

Responses are made on an answer sheet. The question booklet can be used again. The MSI answer sheet is scored by hand using answer keys. Caution needs to be taken to assure that the answer sheet is properly aligned when scoring. Though the question sheet is clear and properly spaced, the answer sheet is too bunched together.

Raw scores are converted into separate T-scores for husbands and for wives. T-scores are appropriate only when the raw scores are normally distributed. Then one could say two-thirds of the norm group scored between 40 and 60; 95% between 30 and 70. Normal distribution seems to be present only with the women's Family History of Distress scale. Nonetheless, the *MSI Manual* advises that scores above 70 are indicative of trouble.

The author claims the 280 questions can be answered in 30 minutes and can be handscored in five minutes.

Location

Snyder, D. K. (1981). *Marital Satisfaction Inventory (MSI) manual.* Los Angeles: Western Psychological Services.

Discussion

The manual shows what a profile would look like if the husband and wife answered each question by responding "true" or by responding "false." In general these couples have T-scores around 60, except for childbearing (about 70) and role orientation (about 40 for those who answer "true" to everything). It is easy to check such response behavior without looking at the manual's sample profiles. Just look at the answer sheet and see if the client tended to answer everything "true" or everything "false."

Studies using the MSI have found that blacks score about seven T-score points higher than whites on all scales except Sexual Dissatisfaction, Role Orientation, and Family History of Distress.

Those with higher education report higher levels of marital satisfaction. Presence of children in the house decreases marital dissatisfaction in the areas of Role Orientation and Children (no surprise here) and also Family History of Distress.

The ability of the MSI to predict posttreatment dissatisfaction after brief directive sex therapy confirms the importance of evaluating nonsexual affection when dealing with sexually distressed couples.

Several small questions remain about the MSI. Granted that the original 440 items were not chosen for their ability to distinguish between therapy clients and the general population. But 271 of the 280 finally chosen did have this (unsought) power to discriminate between the two groups. Why were the remaining nine selected? Another internal consistency study is called for—one that uses no couples in therapy.

The MSI is a promising family questionnaire. For those who find a 280-item inventory too long, the new abbreviated 18-item Disharmony scale was devised for use with the general population, and the 26-item Disaffection scale was devised for use with couples in therapy. It is hoped that more thorough reports about the reliability, validity, and scoring norms of these two new scales will be included in a revised manual.

The manual's chapters on administration, scoring, and interpretation are readable and useful for the practitioner. The chapter on psychometric issues has some items of use for the practitioner but is written in the jargon that earns respect from psychometricians, awe from the general public, and snickers from lovers of English.

The MSI may be purchased from Western Psychological Services, 12031 Wilshire Boulevard, Los Angeles, CA 90025.

Sample Items from the MSI

Conventionalization (CNV)

Reports of a "perfect marriage," 12 items.

70.* There is never a moment that I do not feel "head over heels" in love with my mate.

Reports of a "perfect mate," 9 items.

25. Every new thing I have learned about my mate has pleased me.

Denial of consideration of marital alternatives, 8 items.

88. I have never regretted my marriage, not even for a moment.

Global Distress (GDS)

General unhappiness with the marriage, 30 items.

174. I have known very little unhappiness in my marriage.

Uncertain commitment to the current relationship, 22 items.

152. I am thoroughly committed to remaining in my present marriage.

Affective Communication (AFC)

Complaints of inadequate affection and caring from spouse, 13 items.

238. There is a great deal of love and affection expressed in our marriage.

Experience of lack of empathy and understanding from spouse, 13 items.

21. Sometimes my spouse just can't understand the way I feel.

Failure of spouse to self-disclose, 2 items.

51. My spouse feels free to express openly strong feelings of sadness.

Problem-Solving Communication (PSC)

Minor disagreements become major arguments, 19 items.

129. Minor disagreements with my spouse often end up in big arguments.

Differences remain unresolved or are not discussed, 13 items.

201. During our marriage, my spouse and I have always talked things over.

Spouse is overly sensitive to criticism, 4 items.

54. My spouse has no difficulty in accepting criticism.

Spouse is overly critical and punitive, 5 items.

151. My spouse sometimes seems intent upon changing some aspect of my personality.

Time Together (TTO)

Insufficient time together, 9 items.

227. We just don't get the chance to do as much together anymore.

Lack of common interests, 4 items.

9. My spouse and I don't have much in common to talk about.

Desire for spouse to participate more in respondent's own interests, 4 items.

126. I wish my spouse shared a few more of my interests.

Feelings that spouse does not enjoy time together, 4 items.

236. My spouse seems to enjoy just being with me.

Disagreement About Finances (FIN)

Poor management of finances by spouse, 8 items.

19. My spouse has no common sense when it comes to money.

Financial insecurity as a major source of marital distress, 6 items.

3. Our marriage has never been in difficulty because of financial concerns.

Inability to discuss finances calmly, 6 items.

72. My spouse and I rarely argue about money.

View of spouse as extravagant, 2 items.

200. My spouse buys too many things without consulting with me first.

(continued)

*Numbers indicate the actual number of sample items on the MSI.

Sexual Dissatisfaction (SEX)

General dissatisfaction with the sexual relationship, 11 items.

115. I would prefer to have intercourse more frequently than we do now.

Spouse lacks interest in sex, 8 items.

106. My spouse seems to enjoy sex as much as I do.

Own lack of enjoyment from intercourse, 3 items.

167. I enjoy sexual intercourse with my spouse.

Sexual differences are left unresolved, 5 items.

23. The one thing my spouse and I don't really fully discuss is sex.

Interest or involvement in extramarital affairs, 4 items.

48. I have never been sexually unfaithful to my spouse.

Role Orientation (ROR)

Rejection of traditional marital roles, 12 items.

4. The husband should be the head of the family.

Rejection of the "homemaker" role for women, 7 items.

134. A woman's place is in the home.

Belief in shared home responsibilities, 6 items.

58. A husband should take equal responsibility for feeding and clothing the children.

Advocacy of career opportunities for women, 4 items.

13. A preschool child is likely to suffer if the mother works.

Family History of Distress (FAM)

Parents' marriage dominated by discord, 5 items.

122. My parents had very few quarrels.

Reports of an unhappy childhood, 4 items.

143. My parents never really understood me.

Eagerness to leave home prior to marriage, 2 items.

183. I was very anxious as a young person to get away from my family.

Lack of closeness among family members, 4 items.

17. The members of my family were always very close to each other.

Marital disruption among extended family, 2 items.

204. I certainly hope our marriage turns out better than the marriages of some of my relatives.

Dissatisfaction with Children (DSC)

Children are inconsiderate or disrespectful, 5 items.

273. Our children do not show adequate respect for their parents.

Lack of common interests or activities with children, 5 items.

247. My children and I don't have very much in common to talk about.

Disappointment with children, 5 items.

279. My children consider me an important part of their lives.

Dissatisfaction with demands of childrearing, 6 items.

262. Having children has interfered with pursuit of my own career.

Conflict over Childrearing (CCR)

Childrearing conflicts are a major source of marital discord, 5 items.

258. My spouse and I rarely argue about the children.

Disagreement about discipline, 7 items.

280. My spouse and I rarely disagree on when or how to punish the children.

Unfair sharing of childrearing responsibilities, 7 items.

254. My spouse doesn't spend enough time with the children.

Spouse is uninterested in children, 4 items.

274. My spouse doesn't display enough affection toward the children.

5 | MARITAL AGENDAS PROTOCOL

Clifford I. Notarius and Nelly A. Vanzetti

Introduction

The Marital Agendas Protocol (MAP) is a four-section questionnaire, each section containing 10 or more "agendas" that record the problem areas of the marriage, the level of agreement about the seriousness of the problems, the expectations that the partners have that the problems can be resolved, and whom each partner blames for continued conflict.

Description

The assumption of the Marital Agendas Protocol is that therapy will be effective to the extent that intervention increases the expectancy of success (Bandura, 1977). An index of this expectancy will inform both the partners and the therapist of changes in expectancies.

A problem format is used. Each spouse is asked to consider 10 common issues "all marriages must face": money, communication, in-laws, sex, religion, recreation, friends, alcohol and drugs, children, and jealousy. Room is left for adding other areas. Each partner rates the agenda area on a scale of 0 (for no problem at all) to 100 (for a severe problem). Then, facing the same list, each predicts how the spouse will respond. To measure the belief in possible relational success, the list is presented a third time and each partner is asked "If 10 disagreements arose in this area, how many would you be capable of resolving to your mutual satisfaction?" Finally, each is asked to indicate who is to blame for the unresolved conflicts in each area.

Sample

Eighty-seven couples volunteered to take the MAP and two or three other marital questionnaires.

Reliability

No reliability coefficients are reported.

Validity

The ratings of severity of the 10 problem areas were summed to yield a "problem intensity" score. This problem intensity score showed a strong significant relationship with marital satisfaction (r = –.80 for wives, and r = –.70 for husbands). The estimates of how severely partners would rate each area produced similar results (r = –.82 for wives, r = –.74 for husbands).

Ratings for expectancy of relational success were totaled. This "relational efficacy" score correlated significantly (r = .57) with measures of marital satisfaction and of wives' perceptions of pleasing behavior (r = .32) and communication (r = .41).

The total score for "blaming others" correlated significantly with marital satisfaction (r = –.39 for wives, r = –.55 for husbands). Sum totals for blaming self and blaming both self and spouse do not correlate significantly with measures of marital satisfaction.

Administration

The MAP is a paper-and-pencil test, which can be self-administered in a few minutes. The clients fill out the form separately and do not discuss their answers with each other before completing the questionnaire.

Location

Notarius, C. I., & Vanzetti, N. A. (1983). The Marital Agendas Protocol. In E. Filsinger (Ed.), *Marriage and family assessment: A sourcebook for family therapy*. Beverly Hills: Sage.

Discussion

The Marital Agendas Protocol appears to have face validity and correlates significantly with measures of marital satisfaction. The brevity and simplicity of the instrument would enable it to be used more than once without much effort or threat. Unlike many marital surveys it frames a major part of its questions in terms of expectancies of future behaviors.

Surprisingly, the MAP ignores careers and household tasks as major areas of conflict, although blank spaces are provided for the therapist or clients to add these areas if they wish. The MAP seems to invite imitation and revision, using different items but a similar format.

The sample case brought by the authors suggests that the MAP be used to locate areas of conflict (where a questionnaire may not be necessary) and to explore reasons for low expectancies to resolve the conflict. This use of therapy that is based on expectancy theory calls for a clear description of how this type of therapy is unique and experimentation to demonstrate its effectiveness.

The Marital Agendas Protocol should be considered a research instrument with norms as yet unestablished. Current information on MAP is available from Clifford I. Notarius, Ph.D., Department of Psychology, Catholic University of America, Washington, DC, 20064.

REFERENCE

Bandura, A. (1977). Self-efficacy: Toward a unifying theory of behavioral change. *Psychological Review, 84*, 191-215.

Marital Agendas Protocol

Instructions: Please read each question carefully and record your answers in the spaces provided. Please do not leave any questions blank.

NAME OR ID NUMBER: ______________________ SEX: M _____ F _____ DATE ___________

Question 1a: Consider the list below of marital issues that all marriages must face. Please rate how much of a problem each area currently is in your relationship by writing a number from 0 (not at all a problem) to 100 (a severe problem). For example, if children were somewhat of a problem you might enter 25 below "children". If children were no problem in your relationship, you might enter a 0 below "children". If children were a severe problem, you might enter 100. If you wish to add other areas not included in our list, please do so in the blank spaces provided. Be sure to rate all areas.

MONEY	COMMUNICATION	IN-LAWS	SEX	RELIGION	RECREATION

FRIENDS	ALCOHOL & DRUGS	CHILDREN	JEALOUSY		

Question 1b: How do you predict your spouse will respond to question 1? Enter ratings using the same 0 to 100 scale to indicate how you believe your spouse will respond to question 1. If you added areas to question 1, please add these same areas again and rate each according to how you think your spouse would rate them.

MONEY	COMMUNICATION	IN-LAWS	SEX	RELIGION	RECREATION

FRIENDS	ALCOHOL & DRUGS	CHILDREN	JEALOUSY		

(continued)

Marital Agendas Protocol (*continued*)

Question 2: Out of every ten disagreements in each marital area below, how many do you believe you and your spouse resolve to your mutual satisfaction? Enter a number from 0 to 10 in each of the boxes below. If you added areas, please add them again and rate them also.

MONEY	COMMUNICATION	IN-LAWS	SEX	RELIGION	RECREATION

FRIENDS	ALCOHOL & DRUGS	CHILDREN	JEALOUSY		

Question 3: Who do you feel is responsible for unresolved disagreements in each of the marital areas? Below each area, write "me" if you think that you yourself are primarily responsible for unresolved disagreements, write "partner" if you feel your partner is primarily responsible, or write "both" if you feel you and your partner are equally responsible for unresolved disagreements. Again, if you added areas to the previous questions, please enter these in the spaces provided and rate them also.

MONEY	COMMUNICATION	IN-LAWS	SEX	RELIGION	RECREATION

FRIENDS	ALCOHOL & DRUGS	CHILDREN	JEALOUSY		

6 | McMASTER FAMILY ASSESSMENT DEVICE

Nathan Epstein, Lawrence Baldwin, and Duane Bishop

Introduction

The McMaster Family Assessment Device (FAD) is a questionnaire designed to evaluate families according to the McMaster Model of Family Functioning. Thus, the FAD is made of seven scales: Problem Solving, Communication, Roles, Affective Responsiveness, Affective Involvement, and Behavior Control. The seventh scale, General Functioning, measures the overall health of the family.

Description

Typically, test constructors write a huge number of items, administer them to a large sample, and run the results through a computer. The computer finds groups of questions that are answered by the sample in a consistent way. The various groups of questions or factors are then examined to see what they have in common and, with luck, a proper name can be found to describe each factor. The authors of FAD started with a logical theory, the McMaster Model of Family Functioning. This model conceptualizes six areas of family functioning. For each area 40 items were written. Using the results of individuals who responded to these 240 items, only those items were selected that helped produce as high as possible reliability for each scale and that still helped distinguish each scale from all the other scales. Twelve items were chosen to measure overall family health. These items came from all six scales.

The six scales' content and their final length are:

- Problem Solving (5): the ability to solve family problems;
- Communication (6): the exchanges of information among family members;
- Roles (8): the clear and accepted assignment of tasks and their completion;
- Affective Responsiveness (6): the ability to experience appropriate emotions;

- Affective Involvement (7): the value placed on the family members' concerns; and
- Behavior Control (9): the way the family maintains behavior standards.

The numbers of healthy responses in each of the seven scales are about equal.

Sample

The development of the FAD was based on the responses of 503 individuals, 209 of whom were students in an introductory psychology course. Most of the others were responses that came from members of families who had one member as an inpatient of an adult psychiatric hospital.

Reliability

The internal consistency reliabilities for the six subscales vary from .72 to .83, not very high for anyone using individual counseling, but respectable for short subscales. The General Functioning scale's reliability is .92. No stability scores are available.

Validity

The FAD scores were significantly able to distinguish between individuals who are college students and individuals who have a sibling, spouse, parent, or children in a psychiatric hospital.

A follow-up study using 178 old age (60–69) couples showed that FAD correlated significantly ($r = .53$) with Locke–Wallace Marital Adjustment Test scores and was better than the Locke–Wallace at predicting Philadelphia Geriatric Morale Scale scores.

Administration

The FAD is a 53-item paper-and-pencil test that takes about 15 to 20 minutes for an adult or high school student to complete. Family members rate how each item describes their families by selecting "strongly agree," "agree," "disagree," or "strongly disagree."

Location

Epstein, N., Baldwin, L., & Bishop, S. (1983). The McMaster Family Assessment Device. *Journal of Marital and Family Therapy, 9*, 171–180.

Discussion

The FAD is a recently developed, easy-to-administer questionnaire. It instantly provoked attention because of the theoretical work on which it is based. It is unusual in this computer age to find a "device" whose constructors are proud to ignore factor analysis. If this has helped improve the face validity of FAD, hard work and strong theory do not relieve the authors of the responsibility of finding out if indeed the six subscales are truly six, and if the items have been properly assigned.

Sometimes, the authors try to have their cake and eat it, too. On the one hand, they start with a theory that conceptualizes family functioning with a six-part model. On the other hand, they justify the high intercorrelations between the parts by maintaining that families that are unhealthy in one area tend to be unhealthy in other areas.

Further research is being conducted. As is, clinicians and researchers might add a very short, reliable measure to their screening tool kit, the 12 items of the General Functioning scale.

The McMaster Family Assessment Device

Items are scored Strongly Agree; Agree; Disagree; Strongly Disagree.

Scores per items range from 1 to 4 with 1 reflecting healthy functioning and 4 reflecting unhealthy functioning.

Problem Solving

We usually act on our decisions regarding problems.
After our family tries to solve a problem, we usually discuss whether it worked or not.
We resolve most emotional upsets that come up.
We confront problems involving feelings.
We try to think of different ways to solve problems.

Communication

When someone is upset the others know why.
You can't tell how a person is feeling from what they are saying.
People come right out and say things instead of hinting at them.
We are frank with each other.
We don't talk to each other when we are angry.
When we don't like what someone has done, we tell them.

Roles

When you ask someone to do something, you have to check that they did it.
We make sure members meet their family responsibilities.
Family tasks don't get spread around enough.
We have trouble meeting our bills.
There's little time to explore personal interests.
We discuss who is to do household jobs.
If people are asked to do something, they need reminding.
We are generally dissatisfied with the family duties assigned to us.

Affective Responsiveness

We are reluctant to show our affection for each other.
Some of us just don't respond emotionally.
We do not show our love for each other.
Tenderness takes second place to other things in our family.
We express tenderness.
We cry openly.

Affective Involvement

If someone is in trouble, the others become too involved.
You only get the interest of others when something is important to them.
We are too self-centered.
We get involved with each other only when something interests us.
We show interest in each other when we can get something out of it personally.
Our family shows interest in each other only when they can get something out of it.
Even though we mean well, we intrude too much into each other's lives.

(*continued*)

Behavior Control

We don't know what to do when an emergency comes up.
You can easily get away with breaking the rules.
We know what to do in an emergency.
We have no clear expectations about toilet habits.
We have rules about hitting people.
We don't hold to any rules or standards.
If the rules are broken, we don't know what to expect.
Anything goes in our family.
There are rules about dangerous situations.

General Functioning

Planning family activities is difficult because we misunderstand each other.
In times of crisis we can turn to each other for support.
We cannot talk to each other about the sadness we feel.
Individuals are accepted for what they are.
We avoid discussing our fears and concerns.
We can express feelings to each other.
There are lots of bad feelings in the family.
We feel accepted for what we are.
Making decisions is a problem for our family.
We are able to make decisions about how to solve problems.
We don't get along well together.
We confide in each other.

7 | FAMILY ENVIRONMENT SCALE

Rudolf H. Moos and Bernice S. Moos

Introduction

Social climate is the way an institution maintains or changes itself and provides opportunities for relationships and personal development. Rudolf Moos and his colleagues developed a set of scales to measure the social climate of schools, work settings, correctional institutions, the military, treatment environments, therapeutic groups, and now—the family. The Family Environment Scale (FES) is a 90-item, true-false, self-report questionnaire with 10 subscales designed to measure the social and environmental characteristics of a family.

Description

An initial pool of 200 items was derived from structured interviews with families and from other scales. As a result of the tryout of this experimental scale the FES was developed with nine items for each of 10 subscales. Of these 90 items, 45 were scored true and 45 were scored false. Those items were chosen on which about half of the sample checked "True," half checked "False." Thereby, items that characterized extreme families were avoided.

The 10 subscales and their description are:

Relationship Dimensions

- Cohesion: commitment, help, and support family members provide one another;
- Expressiveness: tendency to act openly and express feelings directly;
- Conflict: openly express anger, aggression, and conflict;

Personal Growth Dimensions

- Independence: the assertiveness and self-sufficiency of family members;

- Achievement orientation: orientation towards achievement and competition;
- Intellectual: cultural orientation-interest in politics, ideas, culture, and social issues;
- Active-recreational orientation: participation in social and recreational events;
- Moral-religious emphasis: stress on ethical and religious activities and values;

System Maintenance Dimensions

- Organization: importance of planning family activities and responsibilities;
- Control: the use of rules and procedures to run family.

There are three parallel forms to FES:

1. The Real Form (Form R), which measures family members' perception of their families of origin or orientation;
2. The Ideal Form (Form I), which measures family members' preferred family environment;
3. The Expectations Form (Form E), which measures the expectations of engaged couples or adolescents about to enter a foster home.

Translations are available in Dutch, German, Hebrew, Italian and Spanish. An abbreviated 40-item Form R is also available.

Sample

The initial pool of items was administered to over 1,000 people recruited by newspaper ads, by contact with students at a local high school, from three church groups, and from minority members contacted by black and Mexican-American research assistants. Some distressed families undergoing treatment were included.

The norms established for the final edition of Form R used 1125 normal families, 294 of which were drawn randomly from specified census tracts in the San Francisco area and the rest from various areas of the United States, various ethnic minorities, and families of all age groups. An additional 500 distressed families comprised the sample, including 220 families of alcohol abusers and 161 families of teenagers in crisis.

Reliability

The internal consistency reliability estimates for the 10 subscales varied between .61 for Independence to .78 for Cohesion, Moral-Religious Emphasis and Intellectual-Cultural Orientation. The median estimate was .73. These statistics were derived from a highly heterogeneous sample.

The test–retest reliability estimates for eight weeks varied between .68 for Independence to .86 for Cohesion. Estimates for 12 months varied between .52 for Independence to .89 for Moral–Religious emphasis. The median test-retest reliability estimates were .78 for eight-week intervals and .73 for 12-month intervals.

Validity

The content of the subscales seems relatively well established as valid. The Cohesion subscale predicts depression and the Cohesion, Recreational Orientation, and Conflict subscales' pretreatment scores are able to predict positive outcomes following therapy. There is a significant correlation between the number of years married and scores on the Independence, Moral–Religious, Active-Recreational, Organization, Conflict, and Expressiveness subscales.

Studies using the FES are mixed concerning their evaluation of FES's correlation with other self-report and observational measures.

FES consistently discriminates between normal and disturbed families and is sensitive to changes in clinic families' environments during treatment. No factor analysis of the FES items has been reported to confirm whether the 10 subscales are indeed independent.

Administration

The FES is a 90-item true-false, self-report questionnaire that can be completed in about 15 to 20 minutes. A reusable booklet is designed to be used with a separate answer sheet. Scoring is a simple clerical task using the overlay template provided. Profiles can be drawn comparing parent-child or husband-wife perceptions or comparing real and ideal family environments.

Location

Moos, R. H., & Moos, B. S. (1981). *Family Environment Scale manual.* Palo Alto, CA: Consulting Psychologists Press.

Discussion

The FES is easy to administer, take, and score. Not all subscales (especially the scale for Independence) are reliable, probably because it is difficult to produce a nine-item subscale that has decent reliability. The profile makes an interesting tool for contrasting real and ideal descriptions of the marriage or differences in perception between the husband and wife. The absence of factor analysis studies and the mixed results when FES scores are compared with other inventory results mean that caution is advised when evaluating "strengths" and "weaknesses" of the relationship.

The manual notes that, when comparing groups, the clinician should be sure to keep in mind such aspects as family size, parent age, and education, which significantly affect FES.

Sample from Subscales of the Family Environment Scale

	Relationship Dimensions
Cohesion:	We really get along well with each other.
Expressiveness:	We tell each other about our personal problems.
Conflict:	Family members often criticize each other.
	Personal Growth Dimensions
Independence:	There is very little privacy in our family.
Achievement Orientation:	Family members rarely worry about job promotions, school, grades, etc.
Intellectual-Cultural Orientation:	Watching TV is more important than reading in our family.
Active-Recreational Orientation:	Nobody in our family is active in sports, Little League, bowling, etc.
Moral-Religious Orientation:	Family members attend church, synagogue, or Sunday School fairly often.
	System Maintenance Dimensions
Organization:	It's often hard to find things when you need them in our household.
Control:	You can't get away with much in our family.

8 | MARITAL ALTERNATIVES SCALE

J. Richard Udry

Introduction

According to Levinger (1979), there are three reasons for marital cohesion: the satisfaction of the marriage itself, the barriers to getting out of the marriage, and the attractiveness of the alternatives to the marriage. The Marital Alternatives Scale is an 11-item questionnaire that measures what it claims to be the thought (usually unspoken) of every married partner, "Could I do any better if I were not married or if I were married to somebody else?"

Description

On each of the items on the Marital Alternatives Scale, the husband or wife responds with a four-point choice: impossible (1); possible, but unlikely (2); probable (3); and certain (4). Nine items are phrased in such a way that the high score indicates the likelihood that a breakup of the marriage would improve the husband's or wife's situation. Two main factors were found, the spouse replacement factor and the economic maintenance factor.

Sample

In 1974, for purposes unrelated to this present scale, a sample of 100 couples were chosen in each of 16 Standard Metropolitan Statistics Areas. They were married, urban, and white, lower and middle income. No religious data were reported. This study was conducted using 375 to 400 couples from this sample who could be traced from 1977 to 1979.

Reliability

The internal consistency reliability estimate of the scale is approximately .70 for each sex, not unusual for short questionnaires, but low for individual counseling. No stability estimates are reported. It is assumed (but not reported) that items h and k were weighted appropriately. They are phrased so that "impossible" rather than "certain" indicates a likelihood of marriage breakup.

Validity

Ten percent of the couples with high Marital Alternatives Scale scores divorced or separated a year after the scale was completed; 18% after two years. Only 1% of the couples with low Marital Alternatives Scale scores divorced or separated after a year; 3% after two years. This difference was significant. The percentages of divorce and separation when one of the couple has a high score and the other a low score are between these two extremes. The percentage of divorce and separation was slightly higher (6% to 4% after one year, 9% to 5% after two years) when the husband's Marital Alternatives Scale score was higher than when the wife's score was higher.

Administration

The Marital Alternatives Scale is a multiple choice, paper-and-pencil questionnaire that takes one to three minutes. Items h and k must be weighted opposite from the way listed (from 4 points for impossible to 1 point for certain).

Location

Udry, J. R. (1981). Marital alternatives and marital disruption. *Journal of Marriage and the Family*, 43, 889-897.

Discussion

When Winston Churchill was asked "How does it feel to be 90 years old?" he is said to have answered, "Very good—when I consider the alternative." Where marital satisfaction questionnaires ask "How happy am I?" they can still imply, "What can I do to become more cohesive with my mate?" The Marital Alternatives Scale, however, basically asks the husband and wife to evaluate divorce or separation.

There are times when questions about divorce and separation are relevant. It is worthwhile noting Udry's finding that, as a predictor of marital disruption, this scale does better than measures of the husband's marital satisfaction. Even for wives, this scale adds significant information that cannot be found in a marital satisfaction survey. There is another case when such a questionnaire might be appropriate: Some spouses do not appreciate the good situation they have because they have not stopped to consider the alternative.

REFERENCE

Levinger, G. (1979). A social psychological perspective on marital dissolution. In G. Levinger & O. Moles (Eds.), *Divorce and separation*. New York: Basic Books.

Marital Alternatives Scale (Wives)

These days it seems like a lot of marriages are breaking up. Of course this isn't likely, but just suppose your husband were to leave you this year. How likely do you imagine each of the following would be? Decide whether you think each item would be impossible, possible, probable, or certain. (Check the appropriate box below.)

How likely is it that:	*Impossible*	*Possible, but Unlikely*	*Probable*	*Certain*
a. You could get another man better than he is?	1	2	3	4
b. You could get another man as good as he is?	1	2	3	4
*i. There are other men you could be happy with?	1	2	3	4
#e. You would be able to live as well as you do now?	1	2	3	4
#g. You would be better off economically?	1	2	3	4
#j. You could support yourself at your present level?	1	2	3	4
##f. You would be able to take care of yourself?	1	2	3	4
c. You would be quite satisfied without a man?	1	2	3	4
d. You would be sad, but get over it quickly?	1	2	3	4
?h. Your prospects for a happy future would be bleak?	1	2	3	4
?k. Your life would be ruined?	1	2	3	4

*spouse replacement
#economic maintenance (for both husband and wife)
##economic maintenance (for husband only)
?The numbering should be reversed for scoring purposes.

9 | INVENTORY OF FAMILY FEELINGS

Joseph Lowman

Introduction

"Iff" is a mathematical jargon word for "if and only if." The Inventory of Family Feelings (IFF) is written without jargon. It is a 38-item, self-report questionnaire that measures one—and only one—dimension of interpersonal and family relationships: the strength of positive feeling. It was constructed with a system in mind and produces scores that map the pattern of the family's positive and, by implication, negative feelings about the family and its members.

Description

A group of 125 undergraduates produced an inventory of 101 items that measured positive and negative feelings towards family members. The items were checked to make certain that they contained words of no more than fifth grade reading level and that other undergraduates agreed that the items were being scored in the right direction.

The responses of 136 family members to the 101-item inventory were analyzed producing a two-factor questionnaire: the Subjective Feelings scale of 23 items, describing feelings towards others, and the Perceived Feelings scale of 15 items, describing how respondents perceive another's feelings towards them. The two subscales correlated so highly with each other (.70) that for most families and research it might be advisable to use the total affect score rather than the Subjective Feelings Scale and Perceived Feelings Scale scores separately.

Five scores are usually produced:

1. *Individual scores* report the rating of one family member by another.
2. *Dyad scores* report the average two family members rate each other.
3. *Response scores* report the average rating an individual gives to members of the family.
4. *Reception scores* report the average rating all other members of the family give each individual.

5. *Family Unit* scores report the average rating of all the Individual scores.

Sample

Reliability data were established using 34 four-member families. Sixteen of these families were selected from mental health agencies in central North Carolina and had two children, one (and typically only one) of whom had been in psychotherapy within the previous year. The other 18 families contained no members with psychological, legal, school, or known marital problems. The children were between the ages of 10 and 21. All subjects appeared average or above average in intelligence. The average education for fathers was 15.3 years. The average age of the fathers was 44.3, of the mothers 42.8, and of the children 15.5. The typical diagnosis for problem children was adjustment reaction of adolescence or childhood neurotic and character disorders.

Reliability

The internal consistency reliability is reported as .98. This phenomenally high reliability is reported on the 101-item inventory. However, using a sample of 34 undergraduates, the stability estimate (after two weeks) for the 38-item IFF is still a very high .96.

Validity

IFF results reported significantly more negative feelings towards emotionally disturbed teenagers than towards nondisturbed children. Significantly more negative feelings were reported from emotionally disturbed teenagers and their fathers than from nondisturbed children and their fathers.

A study of 11 families at New York's Ackerman Institute of Family Therapy found a significant but low negative correlation ($r = -.33$, $p < .05$) between IFF Response scores (positive feelings towards family members) and measures of psychological disturbance. In a study of 20 North Carolina families, a significant positive correlation ($r = .49$, $p < .001$) was found between IFF scores and the Locke-Wallace Marital

Adjustment Test. Satisfied husbands and wives had significantly more positive IFF scores than dissatisfied husbands and wives.

Administration

The IFF is a 38-item, paper-and-pencil inventory that takes less than 20 minutes to complete for a four-member family. Each member of the family answers "agree," "neutral," or "disagree" to each item that describes feelings at that moment towards every other family member. A "neutral" or deliberate nonresponse never receives a point. Rescoring is necessary since half the items are phrased in a negative direction. A chart should be made of each family member's response towards the others.

For example:

	Object of Response				Response Scores
Persons Responding	Father	Mother	Son	Daughter	
Father	–	28	10	28	22
Mother	26	–	13	24	21
Son	8	2	–	15	8.3
Daughter	30	21	16	–	22.3
Reception Scores	21.3	17	13	22.3	Family Unit Score
					18.4

In the above chart the positive feelings the father gives the mother (28), son (10), and daughter (28) are averaged to produce the father's Response score (22), the average expression of positive feelings towards family members *by* the father. The ratings the father is given by the mother (26), son (8), and daughter (30) are averaged to produce the father's Reception score (21.3), the average expression of positive feelings by family members towards the father. All 12 individual responses have been averaged for the Family Unit score.

Charts converting raw scores to percentiles are available to record all of the family dyadic relationships.

Location

Lowman, J. C. (1980). Measurement of family affective structure. *Journal of Personality Assessment, 44*, 130–141.

Discussion

The IFF has a systems approach to reporting family feelings. Its charting system might even gain in value as the family increases in size. Unusual patterns of positive or scapegoating coalitions can be identified. The ability to give and receive affection can be noted. Family Unit scores can compare families. With couples, each spouse can rate parents and in-laws as well as each other, although the IFF is best used with intact family units of more than one child.

What is missing, as Lowman indeed cautions, is the lack of stable norms, especially for scores for children of different ages and for various relationships. The original Subjective Feelings scale and Perceived Feelings scale have been abandoned. They might have had clinical value by revealing lack of communication.

Most people, clinicians included, tend to exaggerate variations in the center of a percentile chart. This is especially true when the chart ignores the normal curve by giving as much space for changes between the 50th and 75th percentiles as for changes between the 75th and 100th percentiles. Thus, a difference of three points at the top of the IFF scale (35 to 38) changes a percentile score from the 95th to the 100th percentile. A similar three-point change in the middle of the scale (26 to 29) changes a percentile score from the 40th to the 65th percentile.

Although the IFF cleverly uses a neutral response choice to elicit nonpositive feelings, human beings still tend to like each other or at least try to say they do. The raw score for the 50th percentile is thus not 19 for this 38-item instrument, but more than 26. It might be safe to view scores as falling within three categories: low (0-23), middle (24-31), and high (32-38).

The simple language means that IFF can be used with less-educated populations. Caution, however, must be taken since the comparison groups that established the percentile norms are highly educated.

Inventory of Family Feelings

Today's Date ____________ Your Name ______________

Instructions

Members of a family feel many different ways toward other members at different times. This Inventory is trying to see how you are feeling about the other members of your family *right now*.

On the following pages are listed 38 statements of how one member of a family might feel toward another member. Beside the statements are six columns. In each are written the letters A--N--D. The "A" stands for Agree, the "N" stands for Neutral, and the "D" stands for Disagree.

1. Please write the name of one of the other members of your family in the space above each of the columns, using as many columns as necessary. You should have a column for each person in your family other than yourself, with any remaining columns left blank.

2. Then, read each item carefully and decide if you mostly feel the same way as the item toward the family member above the first column. If you do, draw a circle around the "A" to show you Agree with the statement. If you do not, draw a circle around the "D" to show you mostly Disagree with it. If you do not feel one way or another towards this person, or if you feel both ways to an equal degree, circle the "N" to show you are Neutral.

3. After marking the first column, go on to the second column and circle "A", "N", or "D", depending on how you feel toward this person. Then go on to the third column and mark it, and so on.

4. After you finish marking all the items on the first page, go on to the next page. Please write the names of your family members in the same order above the columns on every page.

5. There are no right or wrong answers. Try to answer in terms of how you are feeling toward each person *right now*. It is usually best to give your first impression rather than thinking about each item a great deal before answering.

Please mark all the items. It is *very important* that you answer every item. Please check when you have finished to see that you haven't missed any pages. They sometimes stick together. After you have finished, lick the seal on the bottom of the Inventory and fold it over the top. This is to keep your answers private.

Example

	DAD	MOM	BROTHER	______
(1.) I feel close to this family member	(A)--N--D	A--N--(D)	A--(N)--D	A--N--D

If you Agree with this statement (if you *do* feel close to your Dad), circle the "A" in the first column. If you Disagree with this statement (if you *do not* feel close to your Mother), circle the "D" in the second column. If you don't really feel close to your brother, but don't feel distant from him either, circle the "N" in the third column.

(continued)

Inventory of Family Feelings (*continued*)

	Write the names of your family members in as many of these spaces as are needed.					
	______	______	______	______	______	______
(1) I feel close to this family member	A--N--D	A--N--D	A--N--D	A--N--D	A--N--D	A--N--D
(2) I admire a lot of the things about this person	A--N--D	A--N--D	A--N--D	A--N--D	A--N--D	A--N--D
(3) I feel a lot of love for this family member	A--N--D	A--N--D	A--N--D	A--N--D	A--N--D	A--N--D
(4) I feel this family member likes me very much	A--N--D	A--N--D	A--N--D	A--N--D	A--N--D	A--N--D
(5) I like a lot of the things this family member does	A--N--D	A--N--D	A--N--D	A--N--D	A--N--D	A--N--D
(6) This family member doesn't pay a lot of attention to me	A--N--D	A--N--D	A--N--D	A--N--D	A--N--D	A--N--D
(7) I feel a lot of affection for this family member	A--N--D	A--N--D	A--N--D	A--N--D	A--N--D	A--N--D
(8) I don't enjoy being with this family member	A--N--D	A--N--D	A--N--D	A--N--D	A--N--D	A--N--D
(9) I feel wanted by this family member	A--N--D	A--N--D	A--N--D	A--N--D	A--N--D	A--N--D
(10) I am not very thankful to have this person in my family	A--N--D	A--N--D	A--N--D	A--N--D	A--N--D	A--N--D
(11) This family member is usually generous to me	A--N--D	A--N--D	A--N--D	A--N--D	A--N--D	A--N--D
(12) This person has a hard time showing love for me	A--N--D	A--N--D	A--N--D	A--N--D	A--N--D	A--N--D
(13) This family member makes me feel very secure	A--N--D	A--N--D	A--N--D	A--N--D	A--N--D	A--N--D
(14) This person rarely encourages me	A--N--D	A--N--D	A--N--D	A--N--D	A--N--D	A--N--D
(15) I feel like this family member sometimes uses me to get what he (she) wants	A--N--D	A--N--D	A--N--D	A--N--D	A--N--D	A--N--D
(16) I usually feel kindly toward this family member	A--N--D	A--N--D	A--N--D	A--N--D	A--N--D	A--N--D
(17) I could get along all right without this family member	A--N--D	A--N--D	A--N--D	A--N--D	A--N--D	A--N--D
(18) I don't feel very loyal towards this person	A--N--D	A--N--D	A--N--D	A--N--D	A--N--D	A--N--D

Item						
(19) I feel this person doesn't appreciate the things I do for him (her)	A--N--D	A--N--D	A--N--D	A--N--D	A--N--D	A--N--D
(20) I value this person highly	A--N--D	A--N--D	A--N--D	A--N--D	A--N--D	A--N--D
(21) This family member doesn't show a lot of consideration toward me	A--N--D	A--N--D	A--N--D	A--N--D	A--N--D	A--N--D
(22) I feel this person has a lot of love for me	A--N--D	A--N--D	A--N--D	A--N--D	A--N--D	A--N--D
(23) I don't enjoy talking with this person	A--N--D	A--N--D	A--N--D	A--N--D	A--N--D	A--N--D
(24) I don't enjoy listening when this family member is talking	A--N--D	A--N--D	A--N--D	A--N--D	A--N--D	A--N--D
(25) I miss this person a lot when I don't see him or her as much as usual	A--N--D	A--N--D	A--N--D	A--N--D	A--N--D	A--N--D
(26) I usually feel very generous toward this person	A--N--D	A--N--D	A--N--D	A--N--D	A--N--D	A--N--D
(27) This person doesn't have many qualities I would like to have	A--N--D	A--N--D	A--N--D	A--N--D	A--N--D	A--N--D
(28) This person is not usually kind to me	A--N--D	A--N--D	A--N--D	A--N--D	A--N--D	A--N--D
(29) I don't have a great deal of respect for this person	A--N--D	A--N--D	A--N--D	A--N--D	A--N--D	A--N--D
(30) I seldom feel very friendly toward this family member	A--N--D	A--N--D	A--N--D	A--N--D	A--N--D	A--N--D
(31) I feel this person often acts in a selfish way towards me	A--N--D	A--N--D	A--N--D	A--N--D	A--N--D	A--N--D
(32) I don't feel this person is willing to help me in any way he (she) can	A--N--D	A--N--D	A--N--D	A--N--D	A--N--D	A--N--D
(33) I am seldom proud of this person	A--N--D	A--N--D	A--N--D	A--N--D	A--N--D	A--N--D
(34) I often feel very cold toward this family member	A--N--D	A--N--D	A--N--D	A--N--D	A--N--D	A--N--D
(35) I very seldom feel joy when I'm with this person	A--N--D	A--N--D	A--N--D	A--N--D	A--N--D	A--N--D
(36) I feel very warm toward this family member	A--N--D	A--N--D	A--N--D	A--N--D	A--N--D	A--N--D
(37) This person doesn't do a lot to make me happy	A--N--D	A--N--D	A--N--D	A--N--D	A--N--D	A--N--D
(38) I am very fond of this person	A--N--D	A--N--D	A--N--D	A--N--D	A--N--D	A--N--D

Please check to be sure you answered every item on every page. When you have finished checking, seal your Inventory. You are welcome to write any reactions or observations you had about this Inventory in the space below. Thank you very much for your cooperation.

Name ____________

Inventory of Family Feelings
Test Report

Family Member Responding	Family Member Being Rated: Father	Mother	#1	#2	#3	#4	Response Scores
Father							
Mother							
#1							
#2							
#3							
#4							
#5							
Reception Scores							

Family Unit Score ________

INTERPRETATION

This report indicates the amount of positive affect between and among family members. The scale has a range of 0#38, with the high numbers indicating more positive affect.

Response scores represent an average of one member's scores *toward* the others in the family.

Reception scores represent an average of scores that one member *receives* from the other.

A Family Unit score is based on the average individual scores produced by an entire family.

Family Dyadic Relationships

Pairs of members toward each other

Dyads

#1

#2

#3

#4

#5

#6

#7

#8

#9

#10

#11

#12

#13

Percentiles

0%tile 25%tile 50%tile 75%tile 100%tile

Strength of Positive Affect

Raw scores

16 20 22 23 24 25 26 27 28 29 30 31 32 33 1/2 35 38

5

Marital Communication and Intimacy Scales

INTRODUCTION

Failures in communication are almost universal in unhappy marriages. To some extent, marriage and family therapy has grown because it is a communications and intimacy enhancement process. Bienvenu's Marital Communication Inventory (see Measure #10) is a very reliable instrument that measures regard, empathy, discussion, relationship hostility, and self-disclosure in one global score. It is commercially distributed by Family Life. Despite its reliability, critics see it more as a tool for intervention with couples than as a refined research instrument.

Shostrom's Caring Relationship Inventory (see Measure #11) is also commercially distributed (by Educational and Industrial Testing Service). This inventory has five scales: affection, friendship, eros, empathy, and self-love. Self-acceptance might be a better name than self-love. Several subscales overlap.

Schumm, Bollman, and Jurich have drastically abbreviated the Barrett-Lennard Relationship Inventory (see Measure #12). It now is a

13-to-15-item questionnaire that measures level of regard, empathic understanding, and congruence.

Trust frees couples to share feelings. Larzelere and Huston's Dyadic Trust Scale (see Measure #13) measures the trust between the married partners quite distinct from generalized trust. The Dyadic Trust Scale correlates significantly with measures of love and self-disclosure.

Bringle has revised his Self-Report Jealousy Scale (see Measure #14) to measure the tendency of individuals to get upset in nonromantic, minor romantic, and major romantic situations. Jealousy is both a source of intimacy conflict and, for some, a proof of being loved.

Bardis has spent several decades writing questionnaires about marital relationships. The questions generally are appealing, and recently researchers have subjected some of his instruments to psychometric rigors. The Borromean Family Index (see Measure #15) measures nine "forces that attract you to your family" and nine "forces that pull you away from your family." Theorists like Olson (see FACES, Measure #25) view these as the two ends of the concept, cohesion. Bardis believes that in moderation they can be conceptualized as two independent drives.

Waring has come up with an IQ test that might give a different meaning to those initials, the Waring Intimacy Questionnaire (WIQ) (see Measure #16). It is a 90-item, true–false questionnaire that measures emotional closeness, conflict resolution, cohesion, sexuality, self-esteem, compatibility, communication, and autonomy.

10 | MARITAL COMMUNICATION INVENTORY

Millard J. Bienvenu, Sr.

Introduction

"If a married couple are to live together in harmony . . . they must establish honest, uninhibited, and workable systems of communication. . . . Failures and disruptions in communication are almost universal in unhappy and broken marriages. . . . Good communication can be learned and improved upon throughout the life of the couple" (Bienvenu, 1978, p. 1). The Marital Communication Inventory (MCI) is a 46-item, four-point, hand-scored measure of the marital relationship as reported by the spouses.

Description

Bienvenu utilized a review of the literature on marital communication, an examination of existing scales (notably Navran's Primary Communication Inventory, 1967), his own clinical experience, and some pilot studies to produce a 48-item questionnaire. Two items were later eliminated. Later studies revealed several factors, especially relationship hostility and self-disclosure. Other factors found could be labeled "regard," "empathy," "discussion" and, in one study, "conflict management."

Nonetheless, the MCI produces one total score for each of the spouses. Individually, each is required to describe some aspect of marriage with the term "usually," "sometimes," "seldom," or "never." Possible scores range from 0 to 138. Mean scores of about 100 are usually reported with one-sixth scoring about 85 and below, and one-sixth scoring about 120 and above.

Sample

The original studies used 172 married couples. Although the sample is not described, the author resides in northwestern Louisiana and in similar instruments has described his population as predominantly Protestant.

Reliability

The MCI has a high internal consistency, .93. Recent reports have also been high, up to .95. Test–retest estimates have been from .92 for five weeks and .94 for two months.

Validity

Two groups of 23 subjects matched for age, length of marriage, and education were given the inventory. The marital-problems group scored significantly lower than the group with no apparent problems.

Administration

The MCI has an M form for males and an F form for females. The author claims it requires only seventh grade reading ability. The most difficult words are sulk, pout, confidential, semi-monthly, and inventory. Twenty-three items are phrased positively; 23, negatively. The average client takes less than 30 minutes to complete the inventory. Unfortunately, the MCI print is very small and not enough space is given between items.

Location

Bienvenu, M.J., Sr. (1978). *A counselor's guide to accompany a Marital Communication Inventory*. Saluda, N.C.: Family Life.

Discussion

The meaning of the word "communication" can be determined only by the items used. Some items on the MCI reflect the client's lack of communication, others reflect the perception of the spouse's lack of communication. In either case the person's *own* communication score is affected. Does conflict mean poor communication (as in "Do the two of you argue a lot over money?")?

The line between measurement and technique is not always clear. Despite the wide use of the MCI as a research tool (after all, such high internal consistency is hard to find), most critics complain about its lack of validity other than the attractiveness of individual items. Murstein (1978), for example, after criticizing the MCI, admits that it "should be useful as a nonquantitative instrument for guiding and counseling" (pp. 478–479). Schumm, Figley, and Jurich (1979) also feel that the MCI is a much better tool for actual intervention with couples than it is a highly structured and refined research instrument.

The MCI can be purchased from: Family Life Publication, Inc., 219 Henderson Street, Post Office Box 427, Saluda, North Carolina 28773.

REFERENCES

Murstein, B. (1978). A marital communications inventory. In O. Buros (Ed.), *The eighth marital measurements yearbook*. Highland Park, NJ: The Gryphen Press.

Navran, L. (1967). Communication and adjustment in marriage. *Family Process*, *6*, 173–184.

Schumm, W., Figley, C., & Jurich, A. (1979). Dimensionality of the Marital Communications Inventory: A preliminary factor analytic study. *Psychological Reports*, *45*, 123–128.

11 | CARING RELATIONSHIP INVENTORY

Everett L. Shostrom

Introduction

The Caring Relationship Inventory (CRI) is a commercially produced questionnaire that claims to measure the seven "essential elements of love or caring in human relations." The 83-item inventory first measures how each partner sees the relationship and then compares this response to how each partner sees the ideal relationship.

Description

The initial development of the CRI items was guided by the theoretical writings of Fromm, Lewis, Maslow, and Perls. The CRI consists of 83 items: the seven scales, their length, and what they claim to measure are:

- Affection (15 items): helping, nurturing love;
- Friendship (16 items): peer love based on appreciation of common interests;
- Eros (18 items): romantic, jealous, exclusive love;
- Empathy (18 items): charitable compassion and tolerance;
- Self-Love (16 items): to accept one's unique sense of worth in the relationship.

Shostrom then uses some of the above items in new combinations to create two additional scales:

- Being Love (18 items): loving others for the good seen in them;
- Deficiency Love (14 items): loving another for what one can get out of the other.

Shostrom writes that birth to six years is the Eros period, six to 12 is the Empathy period, 12 to 21 is the Friendship period, 21 to 35 is the Affection (Agape I) period, 35 to retirement is the Respect (Agape II) period, and retirement and beyond is the Knowledge (Agape III) period.

Sample

Seventy-five couples who had been married five years or more and who had indicated that they were satisfactorily adjusted served as the norm group. No information is given about these 150 individuals other than their average age (about 36.5 for wives and 38.5 for husbands) and the average length of marriage (about 15 years).

Reliability

No stability data are available. The internal consistency estimates are low for individual counseling but might be acceptable for research (.66 to .89 with a median of .80). The internal consistency reliability for Affection (.76) does not really differ from the correlation between Affection and Friendship (.73) for females.

Validity

According to its manual, CRI scores on Friendship correlate significantly with Person-Person scores on the Pair Attraction Inventory (PAI) (.66 for men, .61 for women). There are significantly high negative correlations between CRI Friendship scores and PAI Confronting Relationship scores (– .41 for men, – .59 for women).

Significant differences on each scale were found between 75 successfully married and 54 divorced couples. Significant differences between 75 successfully married and 50 troubled couples were found on all but the Empathy and Deficiency Love scales.

Administration

A clearly printed answering sheet asks for name, age, occupation, marital status, relationship with person rated, and the number of years in the relationship. On the inventory itself, yes or no answers are given for 83 items. Then the outer edges are folded inwards and the rater rates the 83 items again, this time for the "ideal" other. The examiner needs to check to be sure the booklets are folded correctly.

Scoring time for the seven scales, including rechecking, takes about

five minutes for each person. To score seven scales and four experimental scales and fill in a profile for a couple take about a half hour.

Location

Shostrom, E. L. (1975). *Manual, Caring Relationship Inventory*. San Diego: EDITS/Educational and Industrial Testing Service.

Discussion

The 1975 updating of the 1966 CRI only changes four scale names: Affection (for Nurturing Love), Friendship (for Peer Love), Eros (for Romantic Love), and Empathy (for Altruistic Love). The manual has been slightly expanded.

Although the manual labels one section "Interpretation of the CRI Developmentally," no connection is made between the stages of caring development and the instrument. No evidence is shown, for example, that adolescents will produce higher Friendship scores than Affection scores. Even Freudians might wonder about limiting Eros to those aged six and below. No scale has been developed for Respect and Knowledge scores.

The intercorrelations of some scales are so high that difference scores are meaningless. Shostrom writes, "Concepts measured by the CRI were not conceptualized as representing completely independent dimensions."

The CRI does have face validity for some interesting concepts, but the inventory user will have to combine the Affection and Friendship scores and perhaps the Empathy score.

The CRI may be purchased from: EDITS, P.O. Box 7234, Educational and Industrial Testing Service, San Diego, CA 92107.

Sample Questions from the Caring Relationship Inventory

1. I like to take care of her when she is sick.

11. I have the feeling that we are "buddies" together.

19. I like to tease her.

23. My feeling for her is often purely physical and animally sexual.

52. I feel I can say anything I feel to her.

71. I am afraid to show my fears to her.

80. My relationship with her is characterized by trust.

12 | ABBREVIATED BARRETT-LENNARD RELATIONSHIP INVENTORY

G.T. Barrett-Lennard, Modified by Walter R. Schumm, Stephan R. Bollman, and Anthony R. Jurich

Introduction

The measurement of marital interaction is of special importance to therapists and researchers. The Barrett–Lennard Relationship Inventory (RI) is a 92-item questionnaire that has been used to measure relationships in general. To measure marital relationships in particular an abbreviated version of the RI was constructed.

Description

The RI was devised to measure five aspects of relationships primarily between client and therapist: level of regard, empathic understanding, congruence (the agreement between feelings and the expression of feelings), unconditionality of regard, and willingness to be known. The 92-item questionnaire contained 64 items relevant to marriage relationships. The willingness-to-be-known items and then the unconditionality-of-regard items were eliminated because they were inappropriate to marriage. The six-point response was modified to a five-point "strongly agree" to "strongly disagree" format that has become the pattern used by the majority of marriage inventories. The length of the RI was drastically reduced to increase practicality. The abbreviated RI measures three factors: level of regard, empathic understanding, and congruence between husband and wife. Items that did not relate to these three factors were eliminated.

Sample

Two samples were used: one of 83 couples from rural southeastern Kansas and one of 98 couples from Wichita, Kansas. The middle two-thirds of the couples had been married from 15 to 29 years and had from one to four children. Thirty percent of the husbands and 12% of the wives had graduated from college. Reported income was moderate. Protestants were 62% of the sample; Catholics were 21%; most of the re-

mainder indicated no religious affiliation or did not respond to the religion question. In the two studies 168 husbands and 171 wives responded. These responses were used for the factor analysis.

Reliability

No reliability estimates of the abbreviated RI are reported.

Validity

Other than the factor analysis which eliminated certain items and confirmed three factors, no validity is reported other than the apparent content of the items.

Administration

The abbreviated RI is a paper-and-pencil questionnaire that requires one of five responses from "strongly disagree" to "strongly agree." It takes less than five minutes to complete. A 13-item form could be used for husbands and a separate 15-item form is available for wives.

Location

Schumm, W.R., Bollman, S.R., & Jurich, A.P. (1981). Dimensionality of an abbreviated version of the Relationship Inventory: An urban replication with married couples. *Psychological Reports*, *48*, 51–56.

Discussion

The computer age not only offers an increase in test construction (not an unmixed blessing); it also allows the possibility of evaluating and redoing old tests. The RI originally was intended to evaluate client-therapist relationships from a Rogerian bias. There still might be some use for it with that purpose in mind, but the RI is too long even for researchers. The abbreviated version has some uses, although Schumm (who modified the inventory) should at least report reliability data. Schumm notes that RI items are much less specific than items used in Bienvenu's

Marital Communications Inventory (MCI) (see Measure #10). This might be why Schumm feels that the 46-item MCI is practical for clinical use, although researchers should use the more convenient, short RI.

A copy of the original 64-item, 4-scale form of the RI, including a new adaptation (Form DW-64) for couples, designed to directly tap participant experience of their twosome as such, can be obtained from G. T. Barrett-Lennard, Ph.D., The Centre for Studies in Human Relations, Norwich House, 40 Kings Park Road, West Perth, W. A. Australia 6005.

Abbreviated Barrett-Lennard Relationship Inventory

Directions: For each of the following statements, please indicate the extent to which you agree or disagree with the statement using the following guide and placing the appropriate number to the right of the statement.

1	2	3	4	5
Disagree Slightly	Disagree Moderately	Neither Agree Nor Disagree	Agree Moderately	Agree Strongly

A	10.	My husband (wife) nearly always knows exactly what I mean.	______
A	18.	My husband (wife) usually senses or realizes what I am feeling.	______
A	30.	My husband (wife) realizes what I mean even when I have difficulty saying it.	______
A	34.	My husband (wife) usually understands the whole meaning of what I say to him (her).	______
A	42.	My husband (wife) appreciates exactly how the things I experience feel to me.	______
B	1.	My husband (wife) respects me as a person.	______
B	5.	My husband (wife) feels a true liking for me.	______
*B	21.	My husband finds me rather dull and uninteresting.	______
B	25.	My husband (wife) cares for me.	______
B	37.	My husband (wife) is friendly and warm with me.	______
B	61.	My husband (wife) feels a deep affection for me.	______
C	36.	My husband (wife) expresses his (her) true impressions and feelings with me.	______
C	44.	My husband (wife) is usually willing to express whatever is actually in his (her) mind with me, particularly any feelings about our relationship.	______
C	48.	My husband (wife) is openly himself (herself) in our relationship.	______
*C	52.	There are times when I feel that my husband's outward response to me is quite different from the way he feels underneath.	______

A = Empathic Understanding
B = Level of Regard
C = Congruence
*negatively scored (only included on wife's Inventory)

13 | DYADIC TRUST SCALE

Robert Larzelere and Ted Huston

Introduction

Trust increases security in a relationship, reduces inhibitions and defensiveness, and frees people to share feelings and dreams. The Dyadic Trust Scale is only eight items long yet highly reliable in its measurement of the belief in a partner's benevolence and honesty.

Description

From seven previous scales that measured some type of trust, a total of 57 items were borrowed or adapted. Factor analysis was used to help select items that related highly with each other. The final items were selected to minimize social desirability, to maximize a wide range of responses, and to eliminate repetitiveness. Five items are positive; three are negative. An effort was made to distinguish trust in a partner from the general feeling of trust in mankind.

Sample

A sample of 322 took the test—190 female, 132 male. This sample included 16 casually dating, 90 exclusively dating, 54 engaged or living together, 35 reporting about past dates, 40 newlyweds, 42 longer married partners, and 45 separated or divorced individuals. The dating group had a mean age of 20.8, the newlyweds 23.5, The longer marrieds 35.8, and the divorced 33.0. Most of the dating sample were students in marriage courses at The Pennsylvania State University. The married partners were volunteers from a large number selected at random from the phone book. The divorced or separated partners were volunteers who had just completed another investigation.

Reliability

Internal consistency reliability was .93, very high for an eight-item scale. No test-retest reliability estimates are available.

Validity

The Dyadic Trust Scale does not correlate significantly with measures of social desirability or of generalized trust. It does correlate highly with love scales and moderately with measures of self-disclosure.

Administration

The Dyadic Test Scale is a simple paper-and-pencil, eight-item questionnaire that takes one to three minutes to complete. The taker responds on a seven-point scale from "strongly disagree" to "strongly agree." Total scores range from 8 to 56. The mean score for a separated and divorced sample was 27, for casual dating, 44, for marrieds, 49.

Location

Larzelere, R., & Huston, T. (1980). The Dyadic Trust Scale: Toward understanding interpersonal trust in close relationships. *Journal of Marriage and the Family*, *43*, 595–604.

Discussion

The eight-item Dyadic Trust Scale demonstrates good face validity, high internal consistency, and a respectable correlation with love and self-disclosure. It is not measuring the same thing as generalized trust and social desirability.

The fact that the married partners were all volunteers and the dating individuals were students compelled to participate might have some effect on the scale scores. Yet it must be noted that the divorced participants were also volunteers.

The authors persist in using the term dyad rather than couple. Perhaps the scale can be truly dyadic, that is, used to measure other two-person relationships, like parent–child.

Dyadic Trust Scale

1. My partner is primarily interested in his (her) own welfare.

Strongly Agree	Mildly Agree	Agree	Neither Agree or Disagree	Disagree	Mildly Disagree	Strongly Disagree

2. There are times when my partner cannot be trusted.

Strongly Agree	Mildly Agree	Agree	Neither Agree or Disagree	Disagree	Mildly Disagree	Strongly Disagree

*3. My partner is perfectly honest and truthful with me.

Strongly Agree	Mildly Agree	Agree	Neither Agree or Disagree	Disagree	Mildly Disagree	Strongly Disagree

*4. I feel that I can trust my partner completely.

Strongly Agree	Mildly Agree	Agree	Neither Agree or Disagree	Disagree	Mildly Disagree	Strongly Disagree

*5. My partner is truly sincere in his (her) promises.

Strongly Agree	Mildly Agree	Agree	Neither Agree or Disagree	Disagree	Mildly Disagree	Strongly Disagree

6. I feel that my partner does not show me enough consideration.

Strongly Agree	Mildly Agree	Agree	Neither Agree or Disagree	Disagree	Mildly Disagree	Strongly Disagree

*7. My partner treats me fairly and justly.

Strongly Agree	Mildly Agree	Agree	Neither Agree or Disagree	Disagree	Mildly Disagree	Strongly Disagree

*8. I feel that my partner can be counted on to help me.

Strongly Agree	Mildly Agree	Agree	Neither Agree or Disagree	Disagree	Mildly Disagree	Strongly Disagree

*Reverse scored

14 | SELF-REPORT JEALOUSY SCALE—REVISED

Robert G. Bringle

Introduction

The Self-Report Jealousy Scale—Revised is a 25-item, five-point questionnaire that measures three factors of jealousy: Minor Romantic, Nonromantic, and Major Romantic. The propensity for jealousy is measured in a variety of jealousy-evoking situations. The Revised Scale attempts to eliminate most items that also could be thought to measure envy or rivalry. Jealousy is both a source of conflict and, for some, proof of being loved.

Description

The Self-Report Jealousy Scale was developed to measure individual tendencies to be jealous. It is designed for adult populations. This scale was revised because it described situations that were largely envy situations. Some overlap between envy and jealousy is probably inevitable.

Those who answered the original scale thought the word "jealous" was inappropriate. A frequent comment was, "I wouldn't be jealous, but I would be mad." The word "jealous" was therefore changed to "upset." The option "pleased" presents difficulties to some. The phrase "At least somewhat pleased" could be used to replace it, although no study is reported using this language.

The scale gives five options scored 0 to 4 for each of 25 items. Total scores range potentially from 0 to 100.

The factor analysis of the scale reveals three factors. The main factor includes 14 items (including 11 of the first 14), such as, "At a party your partner hugs someone other than yourself." This factor has been labeled "Minor Romantic." The second factor includes 10 items (including eight of the last 10) such as "Your brother or sister seems to be receiving more affection and/or attention from your parents." This factor has been labeled "Nonromantic." The third factor includes eight items scattered throughout the scale, such as, "Your partner has sexual relations with someone else." This factor has been labeled "Major Romantic."

Sample

The revised scale was first administered to a group of 162 college students. Then it was administered to a second sample of 147 college students and administered to this sample again after two weeks. No demographic data are reported describing these students. In addition, reliable results are reported using a homosexual male sample. This sample was taken before the AIDS crisis.

Reliability

The internal reliability estimates for the whole scale ranged from .88 to .92. Test–retest reliability after two weeks was .77. The internal consistency of the three factors was Minor Romantic, .87; Nonromantic, .80; Major Romantic, .79.

Validity

The validity of the scale was demonstrated by correlating results with other paper-and-pencil measures of what psychologists feel is somewhat connected with jealousy. Thus, those who score high on the Self-Report Jealousy Scale tend to have lower self-esteem ($r = -.36$), are dissatisfied with life ($r = -.46$), tend to be anxious ($r = .36$) and dogmatic ($r = .35$). They see the world in more negative terms ($r = -.25$) and feel they have little control over their own lives ($r = .30$).

These findings are consistent with theoretical expectations, but they obviously dictate caution in counseling the individual. No studies report comparing scale responses of divorced and married couples.

Administration

This is a 25-item, five option, paper-and-pencil self-report. It requires five to 15 minutes to complete.

Several variations are available by modifying the instructions. The instructions can use different language to make the test more specific or general referring to past, present, or future. Even a specific person can be named. The scale is designed for adults. Respondents rate the degree

to which they would be upset if the situations described in the items were to happen.

Location (original scales)

Bringle, R., Roach, S., Andler, C., & Evenbeck, S. (1979). Measuring the intensity of jealous reactions. *Catalogue of Selected Documents in Psychology*, *9*, 23-24.

Discussion

The mean score for 162 college students was 70.62 (standard deviation = 12.75).

To group together sibling rivalry, flirting at parties, and adultery seems to be justified statistically, in the sense that the scale is basically internally consistent. Conceptually, however, these items seem different. After all, income and years of education also statistically go together, and that information may be important in global consideration of socioeconomic class. But money and knowledge are not conceptually identical. Similarly, sibling rivalry and adultery are not conceptually identical. There is, of course, some insight in recognizing that people who remember themselves as jealous children are more likely to be jealous mates. However, it is not clear whether this means that a jealous spouse is likely to exaggerate certain childhood memories.

Self-Report Jealousy Scale—Revised

Below are some situations in which you may have been involved, or in which you could be involved. Rate them with regard to how you would feel if you were confronted with the situation by placing a check mark in a space on the scale. Do not omit any items.

C 1. Your partner expresses the desire that you both develop other romantic relationships.

____Pleased ____Mildly Upset ____Upset ____Very Upset ____Extremely Upset

A C 2. Your partner spends increasingly more time at work with a co-employee you feel could be sexually attractive to your partner.

____Pleased ____Mildly Upset ____Upset ____Very Upset ____Extremely Upset

A C 3. Your partner suddenly shows an interest in going to a party when s/he finds out that someone will be there with whom s/he had been romantically involved with previously.

____Pleased ____Mildly Upset ____Upset ____Very Upset ____Extremely Upset

A 4. At a party, your partner hugs someone other than yourself.

____Pleased ____Mildly Upset ____Upset ____Very Upset ____Extremely Upset

A 5. You notice your partner repeatedly looking at another.

____Pleased ____Mildly Upset ____Upset ____Very Upset ____Extremely Upset

A 6. Your partner spends increasingly more time in outside activities and hobbies in which you are not included.

____Pleased ____Mildly Upset ____Upset ____Very Upset ____Extremely Upset

A 7. At a party, your partner kisses someone you do not know.

____Pleased ____Mildly Upset ____Upset ____Very Upset ____Extremely Upset

A 8. Your boss, with whom you have had a good working relationship in the past, seems to now be more interested in the work of a co-worker.

____Pleased ____Mildly Upset ____Upset ____Very Upset ____Extremely Upset

A C 9. Your partner goes to a bar several evenings without you.

____Pleased ____Mildly Upset ____Upset ____Very Upset ____Extremely Upset

(*continued*)

A = Minor Romantic
C = Major Romantic

A C 10. Your partner recently received a promotion and the new position requires a great deal of travel, business dinners and parties, most of which you are not invited to attend.

____Pleased ____Mildly Upset ____Upset ____Very Upset ____Extremely Upset

A 11. At a party, your partner dances with someone you do not know.

____Pleased ____Mildly Upset ____Upset ____Very Upset ____Extremely Upset

B 12. You and a co-worker worked very hard on an extremely important project. However, your boss gave your co-worker full credit for it.

____Pleased ____Mildly Upset ____Upset ____Very Upset ____Extremely Upset

A 13. Someone flirts with your partner.

____Pleased ____Mildly Upset ____Upset ____Very Upset ____Extremely Upset

A C 14. At a party, your partner repeatedly kisses someone you do not know.

____Pleased ____Mildly Upset ____Upset ____Very Upset ____Extremely Upset

C 15. Your partner has sexual relations with someone else.

____Pleased ____Mildly Upset ____Upset ____Very Upset ____Extremely Upset

B 16. Your brother or sister is given more freedom, such as staying up later, or driving the car.

____Pleased ____Mildly Upset ____Upset ____Very Upset ____Extremely Upset

A B 17. Your partner comments to you on how attractive another person is.

____Pleased ____Mildly Upset ____Upset ____Very Upset ____Extremely Upset

A B 18. While at a social gathering of a group of friends, your partner spends little time talking to you, but engages the others in animated conversation.

____Pleased ____Mildly Upset ____Upset ____Very Upset ____Extremely Upset

B 19. Grandparents visit your family and they seem to devote most of their attention to a brother or sister instead of you.

____Pleased ____Mildly Upset ____Upset ____Very Upset ____Extremely Upset

(*continued*)

A 20. Your partner flirts with someone else.

____Pleased	____Mildly Upset	____Upset	____Very Upset	____Extremely Upset

B 21. Your brother or sister seems to be receiving more affection and/or attention from your parents.

____Pleased	____Mildly Upset	____Upset	____Very Upset	____Extremely Upset

C 22. You have just discovered your partner is having an affair with someone at work.

____Pleased	____Mildly Upset	____Upset	____Very Upset	____Extremely Upset

B 23. The person who has been your assistant for a number of years at work decides to take a similar position with someone else.

____Pleased	____Mildly Upset	____Upset	____Very Upset	____Extremely Upset

B 24. The group to which you belong appears to be leaving you out of plans, activities, etc.

____Pleased	____Mildly Upset	____Upset	____Very Upset	____Extremely Upset

B 25. Your best friend suddenly shows interest in doing things with someone else.

____Pleased	____Mildly Upset	____Upset	____Very Upset	____Extremely Upset

---

A = Minor Romantic
B = Nonromantic
C = Major Romantic

15 | BORROMEAN FAMILY INDEX

Panos D. Bardis

Introduction

Borromeo was the name of a famous Italian family in the Renaissance. Their coat of arms consists of three rings, no two of which are linked. Yet the group of three rings cannot be separated. If any single ring is removed the remaining rings will not be connected. This mathematical model serves not just as the logo for a beer company but as a possible concept of family structure. Families can remain strong when pulled both by forces that attract the individual to the family and by forces that attract the individual away from the family. Two nine-item subscales measure these two connected, yet not interlocked forces.

Description

A survey asked subjects to list the five strongest forces that attracted them to their families as well as the five strongest forces that pulled them away from their families. Separate indexes were constructed for married and for single persons. The final indexes were constructed from the nine most popular pro-family responses and nine most popular anti-family responses.

The theory behind the index is that both independence and family linkage are present to a certain extent in modern societies. The "Borromean family" is one which moderately partakes of both independence and family ties.

Each attraction must be responded to along a five-point range, from 0 (for "absent") to 4 (for "very strong"). The possible range of scores on each half of the index is from 0 to 36. Scores from 13 to 24 are considered in the middle range on both forces that attract and forces that pull away from the family. They can be labeled "Borromean."

Sample

The sample is only vaguely described as large, coming from all or no religions, white and nonwhite, single and married, and from all classes.

Limiting descriptions include the fact that the sample had at least a high school education and primarily came from the Midwest.

Validity and reliability studies used undescribed samples of 28 to 40.

Reliability

The internal consistency reliability estimates for the nine "Forces that attract you to your family" ranged from .88 to .92. The estimates for the nine "Forces that pull you away from your family" range from .79 to .80.

Test-retest reliability for the entire index (for an unspecified period of time) was .90.

Validity

To determine the validity of the index, results were correlated with the Nuclear Family subscale of the Bardis Familism Scale (1959). Correlations were so high (r = .81 to .88) that the two scales might simply be interchangeable for Nuclear Family scores and "Forces that attract you to your family"; similar high negative correlations (r = – .85 to – .93) were found for Nuclear Family scores and "Forces that pull you away from your family."

Administration

The Borromean Family Index is a two-part questionnaire with nine items for each part and a five-point option for each item. The index takes less than 10 minutes to complete and can be answered by teenagers or adults.

Location

Bardis, P. D. (1975). The Borromean family. *Social Science*, *50*, 144–158.

Discussion

The word "Borromean" might appeal to mathematically oriented family therapists, of whom there are few. "Borromean" describes two structures, individualism and familism, which—because they are so prevalent in

our society—perhaps can be conceptualized as two independent drives, at least when found in moderation.

FACES III (by Olson, Portner, and Lavee) (see Measure #25) used factor analysis to produce a single cohesion scale. "Forces that attract you to your family" are enmeshing; "Forces that pull you away from your family" are disengaging. Factor analysis might demonstrate that the Borromean scale is essentially measuring a single factor, family cohesion. No report is given of the correlations of each part of the index with the other. There are no cases of high scores on both parts or low scores on both parts.

The clinician can use the instrument in three ways. First, the items have been selected to show what many people regard to be the nine things that pull families together and the nine things that pull them apart. Second, as in the directions of FACES III, the clients may be asked to describe the family first "as it is" and then "as they would like it to be." Third, clients may be asked to respond to both the index for single persons (which describes family cohesion with family of origin) and the index for married persons (which describes cohesion for family of procreation).

REFERENCE

Bardis, P. (1959). A familism scale. *Marriage and Family Living*, *21*, 340-341.

Borromean Family Index: For Single Persons

This instrument deals with your attitudes and feelings about your own family (father, mother, brothers, sisters). Please read all statements very carefully and respond to all of them on the basis of your own true feelings without consulting any other persons. Do this by reading each statement and then writing in the space provided at its left, only one of the following numbers: 0, 1, 2, 3, 4. The meaning of each of these figures is:

0: Absent.
1: Very weak.
2: Weak.
3: Strong.
4: Very strong.

(Please consider all statements as they are, without changing any of them in any way.)

Forces That Attract You to Your Family

(Remember: 0 means a force does not attract you to your family at all; 1 means the attraction is very weak; 2 means weak; 3, strong; and 4, very strong.)

______ 1. Family love.
______ 2. The fact that we are related.
______ 3. Financial help I receive.
______ 4. Freedom to express myself.
______ 5. My family understands me.
______ 6. Family advice about problems.
______ 7. Physical comforts (cooking, laundry, and so forth).
______ 8. A feeling of responsibility for my family.
______ 9. Companionship.

Forces That Pull You Away from Your Family

(Remember: 0 means a force does not pull you away from your family at all; 1 means the pull is very weak; 2 means weak; 3, strong; and 4, very strong.)

______ 1. Family problems.
______ 2. Friends outside my family.
______ 3. My job.
______ 4. School responsibilities.
______ 5. A desire for financial independence.
______ 6. I want freedom from family control.
______ 7. A desire for privacy.
______ 8. Difference between my ideas and those of my family.
______ 9. Looking for a mate.

You may add a comment concerning your feelings about your family:

(Scoring: the sum of the first 9 numerical responses represents the internal attraction score, while that of the remaining 9 items is the external attraction score. Theoretical range for internal: 0, least pro-family, to 36, most pro-family; external: 0, most pro-family, to 36, least pro-family.)

Borromean Family Index: For Married Persons

This instrument deals with your attitudes and feelings about your own family (spouse and children, if any). Please read all statements very carefully and respond to all of them on the basis of your own true feelings without consulting any other persons. Do this by reading each statement and then writing, in the space provided at its left, only one of the following numbers: 0, 1, 2, 3, 4. The meaning of each of these figures is:

0: Absent.
1: Very weak.
2: Weak.
3: Strong.
4: Very strong.

(Please consider all statements as they are, without changing any of them in any way.)

Forces That Attract You to Your Family

(Remember: 0 means a force does not attract you to your family at all; 1 means the attraction is very weak; 2 means weak; 3, strong; and 4, very strong.)

______ 1. Family love.

______ 2. Physical attraction to my spouse.

______ 3. Common interests.

______ 4. Communication.

______ 5. Companionship.

______ 6. Physical comforts of home.

______ 7. Financial sharing.

______ 8. A feeling of responsibility for my family.

______ 9. My attitude is that having children and caring for them makes a family happier (0 means such an attitude is absent, 4 means very strong.)

Forces That Pull You Away from Your Family

(Remember: 0 means a force does not pull you away from your family at all; 1 means the pull is very weak; 2 means weak; 3, strong; and 4, very strong).

______ 1. Too many social activities.

______ 2. Sexual maladjustment with my spouse.

______ 3. Personality clashes with my spouse.

______ 4. My career or job.

______ 5. Financial problems.

______ 6. House chores.

______ 7. Physical attraction to an outsider.

______ 8. I want freedom from family responsibilities.

______ 9. My attitude is that having children and caring for them is undesirable (0 means such an attitude is absent, 4 means very strong).

You may add a comment concerning your feelings about your family:

(Scoring: the sum of the first 9 numerical responses represents the internal attraction score, while that of the remaining 9 items is the external attraction score. Theoretical range for internal: 0, least pro-family, to 36, most pro-family; external: 0, most pro-family, to 36, least pro-family.)

16 | WARING INTIMACY QUESTIONNAIRE

Edward M. Waring

Introduction

Intimacy problems constitute the largest single cluster of problem behaviors for which outpatients seek psychotherapy. The Waring Intimacy Questionnaire (WIQ) is a 90-item, true–false questionnaire specifically developed to measure the quality of marital intimacy.

Description

The original pool consisted of 496 items chosen for their brevity, content, clarity, ability to discriminate between high scoring and low scoring respondents, comprehensiveness of marital circumstances, freedom from sex bias, and freedom from extreme desirability. Trials on various samples reduced the pool to 10 items for each of the eight facets of intimacy plus 10 items to measure social desirability.

The eight facets of intimacy are:

- Conflict Resolution: ease with which differences are resolved;
- Affection: expression of emotional closeness;
- Cohesion: commitment to marriage;
- Sexuality: sexual needs are communicated and fulfilled;
- Identity: self-confidence and self-esteem;
- Compatibility: ability to work and play together;
- Expressiveness: sharing thoughts, beliefs, attitudes, and feelings; and
- Autonomy: independence from family of origin.

A Total Intimacy score is composed of 40 items, each chosen because it correlates highly with its own intimacy facet but has a low correlation with other facets of intimacy.

Ten items are used to measure Social Desirability.

Sample

The original 496 items were evaluated from the responses of 89 individuals between 18 and 50 who were married. From these, 144 items plus 16 rewritten items were evaluated by the responses of 125 husbands and 127 wives (not necessarily married to each other), 73% of whom were between the ages of 20 and 35; 30% of whom had been married three or less years; and 43% of whom had been married for four to 10 years.

No information is given about race, income, number of children or geographic residence of the sample.

Reliability

The test-retest reliability after two weeks for 152 married individuals varied between .73 and .90 for the eight scales; for the Total Intimacy score it was .89 for males, .86 for females. Internal consistency scores were lower, varying between .52 and .87 for the eight scales. For the Total Intimacy score it was .78 for males and .81 for females.

Validity

The WIQ scales correlated significantly with the Personal Assessment of Intimacy in Relations (PAIR) scales (see Measure #31) except for the Identity scale which PAIR does not measure at all, and the Sexuality scale which correlated only with PAIR's sexual scale. Waring suggests that sexuality may not be a major determinant of marital intimacy, at least as measured by paper-and-pencil tests.

Consistent with the theory of its development, WIQ correlated negatively with measures of nonpsychotic emotional illness and moodiness.

Administration

The WIQ is a paper-and-pencil test. The Social Desirability score is subtracted from the Total Intimacy score to correct for the good impression that the couple was trying to give. The WIQ can be used by noting the profile, the corrected Total Intimacy score, and the discrepancy between the husband's and wife's intimacy scores.

Location

Waring, E. M. & Reddon, J. (1983). The measurement of intimacy in marriage: The Waring Questionnaire. *Journal of Clinical Psychology*, *39*, 53–57.

Discussion

Textbooks constantly tell us that an unreliable test cannot be valid, that is, used for prediction. If you want to guess the grades of a college freshman a year or so in advance, you had better check how consistently the items in your predicting test measure the same thing. For a Total Intimacy scale, Waring deliberately chose 40 items, each of which does not correlate with most of the other items on the scale. This is a nice mathematical way to demonstrate a wide sampling of content, but it might explain why the internal consistency of a 40-item Total Intimacy scale is lower than the internal consistancy scores of some of the 10-item subscores. The technique used to construct nonredundant subscales may have been inappropriate for the Total Intimacy scale.

As Waring himself notes, the validity of the WIQ has been established by comparing results with other paper-and-pencil tests. Comparing results with observer ratings and behavioral measures is both more difficult and more meaningful.

This is a promising questionnaire whose usefulness is still being developed.

6

Special Family Assessment Scales

INTRODUCTION

In addition to global measures of marital happiness and intimacy, specific problems face the client and therapist.

Satisfaction and intimacy imply, at least at first, similarity of lifestyle between husband and wife. However, Dunn, Dunn, and Price's Productivity Environmental Preference Survey (see Measure #17) reminds the couple that, in the words of an ancient sage, "Personalities differ as greatly as do faces." Different preferences for heat or cold, bright light or dim light, high structure or flexibility, late rising or early rising present potential sources of conflict between husband and wife or parent and child. A computer printout might pave the way for tolerance of individual differences.

Since fewer jobs today require gross physical strength and the size of the typical family is closer to two children than four, women are given more time and greater opportunity to reconsider their role. Smith, Ferree, and Miller's The Attitudes Toward Feminism Scale (see Measure #18) revises a prewar inventory by Kirkpatrick to measure the attitudes that can influence male–female roles and relationships in the family.

By 1986 there were 8,545,000 mothers in the working force with children under six (Bureau of Labor Statistics, 1986). Tetenbaum, Lighter, and Travis constructed an Attitudes Toward Working Women Scale (see Measure #19). All but three of the 32 items on the scale concern working mothers. Since women are still "assigned" the prime childrearing responsibilities, tension and conflict may arise even when father and mother both consciously agree about the economic or psychological necessity for the mother to be employed.

The decrease in the size of the typical family, the availability of timesaving tools, and changes in values mean that childbearing and childrearing need not and will not be a mother's main career. Pendleton, Poloma, and Garland's Dual-Career Family Scales (see Measure #20) is a 31-question, six-scale inventory intended primarily for research into self-perceptions of professional women about the roles of wife, mother, and professional.

Booth and Edwards' Marital Instability Index (see Measure #21) has been normed on a highly representative sample. It is a reliable and valid prediction of separation and divorce. The authors claim that if the couple responds "now" to many of the items on the index they indicate that successful therapy is unlikely and divorce counseling is called for.

Straus, in addition to being an important historian, critic, and reviewer of marriage inventories, developed the Conflict Tactics Scales (see Measure #22) to measure how families handle conflict: by reasoning, symbolic aggression, or violence. Family therapists, he feels, should stress reasonable ways of dealing with conflict rather than help families avoid it.

By now, theorists have universally distinguished between aggression and assertion. Aggression seeks mastery over others. Assertion seeks mastery over objects and skills, ultimately mastery over self. The Interpersonal Behavior Survey by Mauger and Adkinson (see Measure #23) measures nine kinds of aggressiveness, 10 kinds of assertiveness, and three kinds of relationship. Three different lengths are available: a brief 38-item screening test, a Short Test of 133 items, and a Long Test of 272 items.

Finally, for therapist trainers, for agencies, and perhaps for feedback, Piercy, Laird, and Mohammed have developed the Family Therapist Rating Scale (see Measure #24). This scale is completed by supervisors or researchers to assess the work of the therapist. It requires less time to administer and interpret than the scales based on the observation of family interaction. (See Chapter 3 for discussion of those techniques.)

REFERENCE

Bureau of Labor Statistics (1986). *Employment in perspective: Women in the labor force (2nd quarter) report 730*. Washington, DC: U.S. Department of Labor.

17 | PRODUCTIVITY ENVIRONMENTAL PREFERENCE SURVEY

Rita Dunn, Kenneth Dunn, and Gary Price

Introduction

It has long been known that there are important differences between two people who constitute a couple, whether married or about to be married. The Productivity Environmental Preference Survey (PEPS) is a 100-item inventory that helps identify individual adult preferences in 20 kinds of working, learning, or home environments. Differences in these preferences are potential sources of conflict in family living. For example, "I like it warm; you like it cool," or "Children should study only with absolute quiet; children want a loud stereo blasting."

Description

The Productivity Environmental Preference Survey (PEPS) evolved from prior inventories. The Learning Style Inventory (1975) was constructed in an effort to find environments and structures that would help individualize instruction in elementary and high school. It was found that individualized environments improved learning.

Then Dunn, Dunn, and Price developed the PEPS for adults. At first, PEPS measured 21 different elements selected by content and factor analysis. These elements identified how adults prefer to function in the following areas:

(a) immediate environment—
no sound/soft music/noise,
bright light/dim light,
warmth/cold,
formal design/informal design;

(b) emotionality—
well motivated/hard to motivate,
persistent/nonpersistent,
responsible/irresponsible,
highly structured/flexible;

(c) sociological needs—
self-oriented/colleague-oriented/authority-oriented/oriented in varied ways; and

(d) physical needs—
perceptual preference (hearing/seeing/feeling/kinesthetic), requires intake (chewing or eating)
time preference (morning/evening/late morning/afternoon), needs mobility.

The self-oriented and colleague-oriented ways of learning were later combined.

In response to a tryout, certain items were reconstructed to elicit a greater variety of responses and a five-point scale (from "strongly agree" = 5 to "strongly disagree" = 1) replaced the original true-false scale.

Sample

The revision of the PEPS was based on a nonrandom sample of 589 adults from several states and from various academic and industrial settings. No further description of this sample is given.

Various research studies that could contribute to proof of the validity of the PEPS seem to have been conducted mainly on students at the University of Kansas in Lawrence and St. John's University in New York City.

Reliability

The manual reports internal consistency reliability estimates for the PEPS using the unrevised edition. Some of these reliabilities (sound, light, responsibility, learns alone, auditory preferences, requires intake, and needs mobility) are respectable, .82 to .87. Some of these reliability estimates (for warmth, persistence, structure, kinesthetic preferences, and prefer to function in the afternoon) were so low (.29 to .47) that the questions had to be revised and the five-point scale constructed.

The intercorrelation coefficients are respectably low. This means that the survey does possess unique areas. Only seven of the 210 inter-correlations are .25 or above. Persistence, responsibility, and motivation relate perhaps too highly with each other to be considered separate scales.

Validity

PEPS primarily has only face validity. However, the authors did combine both testing and research. Among findings that might constitute construct validity are the ability of authority-oriented, motivation, auditory preference (listening to lectures?), and morning and afternoon time preference scales to predict graduate school grade point average. The elderly preferred (more than undergraduates) not to work in the afternoon. Women preferred more warmth than men. Students indicated greater responsibility as they got older.

Administration

PEPS takes about a half hour to complete and is scored by computer. A five-point scale from "strongly agree" to "strongly disagree" is used. Clients are asked to answer as quickly as possible. Interviews are often valuable in administering the survey. Computer scoring and profiles are available.

Location

Price, G., Dunn, R., & Dunn, K. (1982). *Productivity Environmental Survey manual*. Lawrence, KS: Price Systems Inc.

Discussion

PEPS, the first comprehensive approach to the diagnosis of an adult's individual productivity, is still being developed. The manual indicates that the authors are aware of a constant need to go back to the drawing board. It is possible that the low reliability of some intriguing subscales is the result of the small number of items used in these scales rather than simply a sign that the items need to be rewritten.

The instructions to answer the questions as quickly as possible are based on the assumption that the first, unrationalized answer is the best. The survey manual should include a stability coefficient to prove this assertion.

Recently, the authors used PEPS to measure married couples. Compatability includes not only values and interests but also productivity styles. This is not to say that minor differences should be determining factors. Nonetheless, White and Hatcher (1984) caution that there is more evidence of the relationship between similarity and couple satisfaction than between complementarity and satisfaction. It may be necessary for the therapist to show—and how better than with a computer printout—that if he prefers to work with music and she likes it quiet, or he likes to go to bed at 11:00 and she at 1:00, these choices may not be made just to get on the spouse's nerves. A clinical example: one husband who ignored oral reminders quickly responded to a written one. The PEPS explanation: he needed a visual presentation, not an auditory one. At least, therapists can hope that reworking and continued research can add a reliable and valid as well as fascinating survey to their toolkit. PEPS may be purchased from: Price Systems, Inc., Box 3067, Lawrence, KS 66044.

REFERENCES

Dunn, R., Dunn, K., & Price, G. (1975). *Learning Style Inventory*. Lawrence, K. S.: Price Systems Inc.

White, S., & Hatcher, C. (1984). Couple complementarity and similarity: A review of the literature. *American Journal of Family Therapy, 1*, 15-25.

Productivity Environmental Preference Survey

Directions:

This Productivity Survey has several statements about how adults prefer to function, learn, concentrate and perform their occupational or educational tasks. Read each statement and decide to what degree you would agree or disagree with that statement. If you strongly agree mark SA, if you strongly disagree mark SD. If neither of the above options best describes how you feel, indicate the option between SD and SA that does describe how you feel most of the time.

Give your immediate or first reaction to each question. Please answer each question on the separate answer sheet. Do not write on this booklet.

Before you begin to answer the questions; write your name, sex, date of birth, and any other information requested in the space provided on the answer sheet using a no. 2 pencil (blacken the bubbles below each of the boxes you filled out on the answer sheet).

Please answer all the questions.

P.O. Box 3067, Lawrence, Kansas 66044

Productivity Environmental Preference Survey (*continued*)

1. I prefer working in bright light.
2. I like to work alone.
3. It is easy for me to concentrate late at night.
4. I like to draw or use diagrams when I work.
5. I often have to be reminded to complete certain tasks or assignments.
6. The one job I like doing <u>best</u>, I do with an expert in the field.
7. I can think better lying down than sitting.
8. I prefer cool temperatures when I need to concentrate.
9. I can block out noise or sound when I work.
10. People keep reminding me to do things.
11. It is difficult for me to concentrate when I am warm.
12. The one job I like doing <u>best</u>, I do with two or more people.
13. I often work in an area where the lights are low.
14. When I concentrate I like to sit on a soft chair or couch.
15. I usually finish what I start.
16. The things I remember best are the things that I hear.
17. I enjoy tasks that allow me to take breaks.
18. I can work more effectively in the afternoon than in the morning.
19. I like to "snack" when I' m concentrating.
20. When I really have a lot of work to do I like to get it done with several colleagues.
21. Noise or extraneous sound usually keeps me from concentrating.
22. I often forget to do the things I' ve said I would do.
23. I enjoy working with my hands.
24. I like to work or analyze an assignment with another individual.
25. I prefer cool temperatures when I' m working.
26. The one job I like doing <u>best</u>, I do with several people.
27. I concentrate best in the late afternoon.
28. The things I remember best are the things that I see or read.
29. I usually complete tasks that I start.
30. I think best sitting up.
31. I like to learn or work with an expert.
32. I work best early in the morning.
33. I get a lot done when I work on my own.
34. When I work I turn all the lights on.
35. I prefer that others share responsibility for a task we' re doing.
36. I really enjoy television.
37. I like having access to supervisors when I have an important task to complete.
38. I like to sit on a straight-back chair when I concentrate.
39. I work or study best by myself.
40. I can remember things best when I study them in the evening.
41. The things I remember best are the things that I see in a movie, book, magazine, photo or diagram.
42. I always finish tasks that I start.
43. If I have to learn something new, I prefer to learn about it by hearing a record, a tape, or a lecture.
44. I am most alert in the evening.
45. The one job I like doing <u>best</u>, I do with a group of people.
46. I am uncomfortable when I work or try to study in a warm room.
47. I prefer to have deadlines when I work.
48. I like to eat while I' m concentrating.
49. I prefer completing one thing before I start something else.
50. It is difficult for me to get started on a new task.

(*continued*)

Productivity Environmental Preference Survey (*continued*)

51. I really enjoy movies.
52. I have to be reminded to do things I' ve said I would do.
53. I work best when the lights are low.
54. When I have a great deal of work to do I prefer that supervisors stay away until my work has been completed.
55. I keep trying to accomplish a task even if it appears that I may not succeed.
56. I like to learn about something new by hearing a tape or a lecture.
57. I feel I am self-motivated.
58. The one job I like doing best, I prefer doing alone.
59. Eating something would distract me when I' m working.
60. My performance improves if I know my work will be checked.
61. I prefer to work with music playing.
62. I stay at a task until it is finished.
63. I learn best by doing on the job.
64. I gain a great deal of satisfaction from doing the best I can.
65. I remember how to do a new task when I learn it step by step.
66. I often read in dim light.
67. If I have to learn something new, I like to learn about it by seeing a film-strip, photographs, or diagrams.
68. I like others to outline very carefully what they want me to do.
69. I would rather start work in the morning than in the evening.
70. I constantly change positions in my chair.
71. The things I remember best are the things that I hear.
72. I like my instructor(s) or supervisor(s) to recognize my efforts.
73. I learn better by reading than by listening to someone.
74. I get more done in the afternoon than in the morning.
75. I can block out most sound when I work.
76. I really like to build things.
77. I prefer to work under a shaded lamp with the rest of the room dim.
78. I choose to eat, drink, smoke or chew only after I finish working.
79. I remember things better when I study in the evening.
80. If I have to learn something new, I like to learn about it by seeing a movie.
81. I feel good when my spouse, colleague or supervisor praises me for doing well at my job.
82. I prefer a cool environment when I try to study.
83. It' s difficult for me to block out sound (music, T.V., talking) when I work.
84. I would rather learn by experience than by reading.
85. I like being praised for a "job well done."
86. It' s difficult for me to sit in one place for a long time.
87. I work best if coffee is available.
88. I enjoy doing experiments.
89. If a task becomes very difficult, I tend to lose interest in it.
90. I enjoy learning new things about my work.
91. I can sit in one place for a long time.
92. I can concentrate best in the evening.
93. I prefer to study with someone who really knows the material.
94. I often change my position when I work.
95. I would work more effectively if I could eat while I' m working.
96. If I can go through each step of a task, I usually remember what I learn.
97. I learn better when I read the instructions than when someone tells me what to do.
98. I only begin to feel wide awake after 10:00 A.M.
99. I often complete unfinished work on a bed or couch.
100. I often wear a sweater or jacket indoors.

18 | ATTITUDES TOWARD FEMINISM SCALE

Eliot R. Smith, Myra Marx Ferree, and Frederick D. Miller

Introduction

By 1985, less than 4% of American workers were involved with farming, and less than 25% were involved in manufacturing products (U.S. Bureau of the Census, 1986). The postindustrial, service-centered economy has arrived. Zero population growth has become a societal ideal. These two facts—fewer jobs requiring gross physical strength and the emergence of smaller families—contributed greatly to a changing economic and family role for women. The changing roles furthered the development of the Women's Movement, which has affected all human relationships, including the family.

The Attitudes Toward Feminism Scale (FEM) is a 20-item inventory with five response alternatives. It measures the acceptance or rejection of the central beliefs of feminism rather than attitudes towards avowed feminists. These attitudes can influence male-female roles and relationships in the family and the family's interaction with society.

Description

In 1936, Kirkpatrick wrote the Belief Pattern Scale for Measuring Attitudes Toward Women. This scale had 50 items and had little use when it was first constructed. Although others have recently attempted to write feminism inventories, the Kirkpatrick scales still retain a clarity and brevity, plus a solid statistical background. The FEM is a revision of the Kirkpatrick Belief Pattern Scale.

The first draft of the FEM used 41 items of Kirkpatrick's scale that were deemed still usable in the original or in modified form. Sixteen items were developed to capture the modern spirit: for example, "Whether or not they realize it, most women are exploited." Items were discarded if they evoked similar responses from pro-feminists and anti-feminists, such as, "A working wife has no more right to alimony from her husband than he has right to alimony from her." Items that evoked a narrow variation of responses were eliminated. Various trials reduced the scale to 20 items. Sixteen items are negatively phrased. Eight items are taken from Kirkpatrick; five are modified Kirkpatrick items.

Sample

The FEM scale was first tested on an undergraduate Ivy League college psychology course with 28 males and 11 females. The second scale (by now reduced to 27 items) was tested on 52 female and 48 male Harvard Summer School students.

Reliability

The internal consistency reliability estimate of the 20-item scale was .91. No stability estimates are reported.

Validity

FEM scores correlate highly (.63) with a paper-and-pencil measure of the subject's identification with the Women's Movement. It has a moderate but significant (.39) correlation with self-reports of actual participation in feminist events. It has a low but significant correlation (.24) with a paper-and-pencil inventoried belief in an unjust world. Factor analysis shows that the FEM measures a single factor which the authors naturally label "Feminism."

Administration

The FEM scale is a 20-item, paper-and-pencil inventory with five response alternatives from "strongly agree" to "strongly disagree." It can be completed in approximately five minutes.

Location

Smith, E. R., Ferree, M. M., & Miller, F. D. (1975). A Short Scale of Attitudes Toward Feminism. *Representative Research in Social Psychology*, *6*, 57–62.

Discussion

Conflict over the roles that husbands and wives are supposed to play is a section in numerous marital scales. Unlike measurements of communication or sexual satisfaction there is some conflict on how to score attitudes towards feminism. Using a Lutheran population, at least, pro-feminism is related to lack of marital satisfaction. Pro-feminist, pro-family counselors are left with the following conclusions: feminism is an issue of conflict in our society and can be a source of conflict in some families. There is a feeling, which needs to be checked by research, that it is less important to marital happiness if both the husband and wife are either pro- or anti-feminist. What is important is the agreement between the husband and wife on this increasingly important area. The FEM, however, is more political and social than familial. It does not ask, "Who gets up at 3 A. M. to feed the baby?" or "Who cleans the house?"

REFERENCES

Kirkpatrick, C. (1936). Measuring attitudes toward feminism. *Sociology and Social Research*, *20*, 512–526.

U.S. Bureau of the Census (1986). *Statistical abstract of the United States, 1986* (106th Edition). Washington, DC: U.S. Government Printing Office.

The Attitudes Toward Feminism Scale (FEM)

Directions: For each statement, please indicate the extent to which you agree or disagree with the statement using the following guide and placing the appropriate number to the right of the statement.

Strongly Agree (1)
Agree (2)
Neither Agree Nor Disagree (3)
Disagree (4)
Strongly Disagree (5)

1. Women have the right to compete with men in every sphere of activity.** ______
2. As head of the household, the father should have final authority over his children.* ______
3. The unmarried mother is morally a greater failure than the unmarried father.* ______
4. A woman who refuses to give up her job to move with her husband would be to blame if the marriage broke up. ______
5. A woman who refuses to bear children has failed in her duty to her husband.* ______
6. Women should not be permitted to hold political offices that involve great responsibility.* ______
7. A woman should be expected to change her name when she marries.** ______
8. Whether or not they realize it, most women are exploited by men. ______
9. Women who join the Women's Movement are typically frustrated and unattractive people who feel they lose out by the current rules of society. ______
10. A working woman who sends her six month old baby to a daycare center is a bad mother. ______
11. A woman to be truly womanly should gracefully accept chivalrous attentions from men.* ______
12. It is absurd to regard obedience as a wifely virtue.* ______
13. The "clinging vine" wife is justified provided she clings sweetly enough to please her husband.* ______
14. Realistically speaking, most progress so far has been made by men and we can expect it to continue that way. ______
15. One should never trust a woman's account of another woman.* ______
16. It is desirable that women be appointed to police forces with the same duties as men.** ______
17. Women are basically more unpredictable then men. ______
18. It is all right for women to work but men will always be the basic breadwinners. ______
19. A woman should not expect to go to the same places or have the same freedom of action as a man.** ______
20. Profanity sounds worse generally coming from a woman.** ______

*Item drawn from Kirkpatrick. **Item modified from Kirkpatrick.

19 | ATTITUDES TOWARD WORKING WOMEN SCALE

Toby J. Tetenbaum, Jessica Lighter, and Mary Travis

Introduction

In 1960, fewer than 3,000,000 women with children under age six (14% without spouse present) were in the labor force (U.S. Bureau of Census, 1986). By March 1986, this number had risen to 8,545,000 (23% without spouse present) (U.S. Bureau of Labor Statistics, 1986). And a baby boom is expected for the remainder of the decade. Child developmentalists have expressed concern about what happens to the mother-infant relationship when the mother, who is still "assigned" the prime childrearing responsibilities, is employed. Changes in women's roles inevitably lead to changes in men's roles or to tension and conflict. The Attitudes Toward Working Women Scale is a 32-item, seven-point inventory that measures the attitude towards working mothers.

Description

A 45-item rating scale was devised to measure the attitudes towards working mothers and the effect of women's work on the women and their families. Thirty-two items were negatively phrased and 13 positively phrased. The 32 items were retained because they measured the same thing. Scoring was done on a seven-point rating from 1 for "disagree strongly" to 7 for "agree strongly."

Sample

The original sample was 526 students attending the graduate school of Education of Fordham University, a New York City Catholic-run institution with a variety of faiths represented in the student body. Of these 45% were teachers, 18% counselors and school psychologists, and 15% administrators. About two-thirds were female, two-thirds were between the ages of 21–35, and the rest were older. Approximately 44% were single (including 4% nuns), 48% were married, and 8% divorced, separated, or widowed. Nonwhites constituted 30% of the sample.

Later validity studies included 81 NOW members and 73 Right-to-Life anti-feminists from a New York suburb.

Other validity studies involved another 60 graduate students not included in the original study and 330 educators in the suburbs north of New York City, 128 suburban white 11th- and 12th-graders, and 68 lower-class, urban Hispanic high school students.

Reliability

No internal consistency reliability estimates are reported for the whole 45 items. After 13 items were discarded for reducing the internal consistency, reliability of .94 for females and .95 for males for the remaining items were reported. No further tests of reliability using this new 32-item scale were reported, so these reliability scores can be assumed to be higher than another test of reliability would show.

Validity

Right-to-Life women scored more than twice as conservatively as NOW women. Working NOW and Right-to-Life women were significantly more liberal than nonworking women in these groups. Men were significantly more conservative than women, Hispanic students somewhat more conservative than white suburban students. Although the scales correlated significantly with measures of attitudes towards feminism or towards the traditional feminine role, none of these correlations was higher than .25, demonstrating that attitude towards women working is meaningful in its own right.

Administration

The scale is administered and scored by hand. It takes about 15 minutes to complete. All 45 original questions are administered to minimize the tendency to answer all questions the same way, but the 13 positive items are not included in the final score. It is important to check directions before administering and grading.

c'
.ıbaum, T. J., Lighter, J., & Travis, M. (1981). Educator's atti-
es toward working mothers. *Journal of Educational Psychology*, *73*, 369-375.

Discussion

The face validity of this instrument may upset some users. If all positively phrased items are not to be scored because they are not consistent with the total score, might not this be the result of the original sample containing three times as many items that were negatively phrased as had been positively phrased? If the ratio had been reversed, perhaps the scale would have ended up selecting 32 positively phrased items.

Of course, clients are usually resilient enough to tolerate the language tilt of this scale. Yet, if there are conflicts over the mother's employment within the family, this scale's language may upset some women. Perhaps that is why, despite the high reliability and respectable validity, the authors recommend the scale for research and say not a word about marital therapy.

The scale may reveal working mothers' feelings of guilt about briefly leaving their children. Especially if the reason for employment is economic necessity, despite the conscious agreement that the wife must work, there may remain a feeling on the part of the husband that a working wife is to some extent not quite right. This scale can bring out these feelings for honest discussion.

REFERENCES

U.S. Bureau of Census (1986). *Statistical abstract of the United States, 1986* (106th edition). Washington, DC: U.S. Government Printing Office.

U.S. Bureau of Labor Statistics (1986). *Employment in perspective: Women in the labor force (2nd quarter) report 730.* Washington, DC: U.S. Department of Labor.

Attitudes Toward Working Women Sc.

(Administer as is [i.e., all 45 items] to keep response set from occurring bu 4, 8, 12, 16, 17, 20, 24, 28, 32, 35, 36, 40, 45 when summing the remainin items are administered but only 32 are tallied.)

Directions: The statements below reflect a number of different opinions and points o probably find that you agree with some of these statements and disagree with othe statement, please indicate the extent to which you agree or disagree with the statemen following guide and placing the appropriate number to the left of the statement.

1	2	3	4	5	6	7
Disagree Strongly	Disagree Moderately	Disagree Slightly	Neither Agree Nor Disagree	Agree Somewhat	Agree Moderately	Agree Strongly

There are no right or wrong answers so answer as honestly as you can, according to your *opinion*. Please consider each statement separately but don't spend too much time on any one statement. Try to answer as best you can, and then go on.

_____ 1. Mothers should be home when their children return from school.
_____ 2. Working mothers can't be as close to their children as non-working mothers.
_____ 3. No matter how good the quality of a hired domestic or baby-sitter, it can never compare to the care of a mother.
_____ 4.* Working mothers are generally more interesting than non-working mothers.
_____ 5. Children of non-working mothers generally get into less trouble than children of working mothers.
_____ 6. Households of working women do not run as smoothly as households of non-working women.
_____ 7. Children are a more important priority of non-working mothers than working mothers.
_____ 8.* Women should not sacrifice their chance for a career just to be home with their children.
_____ 9. A woman who wants to work should try to find a job that matches her child's school schedule.
_____ 10. Children of non-working mothers feel more loved than children of working mothers.
_____ 11. Working women tend to be overly aggressive and competitive.
_____ 12.* It's beneficial for a child to have a working mother because the child learns self-reliance and responsibility.
_____ 13. Non-working mothers spend more time interacting with their children than working mothers.
_____ 14. Children of working mothers watch more T.V. than children of non-working mothers.
_____ 15. Mothers who stay home are in a better position to supervise their children's choice of friends than mothers who go to work.
_____ 16.* Women owe it to themselves to pursue a career if they want to, even if they have children.
_____ 17.* You can't pay another person to do what a mother will do for free.
_____ 18. The money a working mother earns can't be worth what it costs in its negative effects on the child.
_____ 19. Children of working mothers require more attention from their teachers than children of non-working mothers.
_____ 20.* In the long run, children grow up and leave home, and a mother will have wasted the best years of her life if she stays home for them instead of pursuing a career.

(*continued*)

1	2	3	4	5	6	7
Disagree Strongly	Disagree Moderately	Disagree Slightly	Neither Agree Nor Disagree	Agree Somewhat	Agree Moderately	Agree Strongly

_____ 21. Mothers who stay home tend to be more patient and warmer than mothers who go to work.
_____ 22. To compensate for their time away from home, working mothers often spoil their children.
_____ 23. Children of working mothers are sent to school when they are sick (i.e., colds, runny nose, stomach ache) more often than children of non-working mothers.
_____ 24.* Most children of working mothers are proud that their mothers work.
_____ 25. Children of working mothers may seem more independent than children of non-working mothers, but they are actually more insecure.
_____ 26. If a woman decides to have children, she owes it to them to stay home with them at least until they're of school age.
_____ 27. Women who stay home are more consistent in disciplining their children than mothers who work.
_____ 28.* Even though the working mother may have less time with her children than the non-working mother, the quality of the relationship is probably as good or better.
_____ 29. No matter how well the child of a working mother seems to be handling things now, the harmful effects on her family are bound to show up at some point.
_____ 30. While women sometimes have to work, they really belong in the home.
_____ 31. Non-working mothers stay on top of their child's day-to-day school performance more than working mothers.
_____ 32.* Because of their experiences out in the world, working mothers are better able to bring up their children for today's world than non-working mothers.
_____ 33. Part-time work gives a mother a change she might feel she needs, but full-time work is too disruptive to the family.
_____ 34. Children are only young once and it is unfair to place home and child care responsibilities onto an older child just because the mother wants to work.
_____ 35.* No woman, no matter how bright, energetic and capable, can have a family and a career and do both well.
_____ 36.* Working mothers are more attractive to their husbands than non-working mothers.
_____ 37. Mothers who have to work should find jobs that allow them to work at home.
_____ 38. In the rush of getting their families and themselves out in the morning, working mothers sometimes send their children to school more untidy than nonworking mothers.
_____ 39. Working mothers can be so preoccupied with their jobs that even when they are home, their minds aren't on their families.
_____ 40.* Young girls whose mothers work are lucky to have such a good example to pattern themselves after.
_____ 41. Women who stay home are more effective in disciplining their children than mothers who work.
_____ 42. Women who work often put an unfair burden on neighbors, friends and relatives for the care of their children.
_____ 43. The recent high divorce rate can be directly related to mothers going back to work.
_____ 44. Mothers who go to work have to expect their children to feel somewhat abandoned and resentful.
_____ 45.* The difficulties women face in trying to raise children, run a home and also work make them deserving of as much support from everyone as possible.

*Items not tallied in score.

20 | DUAL-CAREER FAMILY SCALES

Brian F. Pendleton, Margaret M. Poloma, and T. Neal Garland

Introduction

Traditionally, the husband has been the family breadwinner. There was no need to ask a woman raising a half a dozen children what she did. The question was, how could she do it? The decrease in the size of the typical family to one to three children, the availability of timesaving tools, and changes in values mean that childbearing and childrearing need not and will not be the mother's main career. The Dual-Career Family Scales is a 31-question, six-scale inventory intended for research into self-perception of professional women about the roles of wife, mother, and professional.

Description

In 1969, separate but simultaneous interviews were conducted with 53 couples. Based on these interviews a questionnaire was developed and sent, in 1977, to the wives who had participated.

The items for each of the scales are ordered according to difficulty. That is, more wives found the first item under each scale name easiest to agree with. There are six scales chosen not by the responses of the wives but by the intuition of the researcher. The scale names, number of items, and content are:

- Marriage Type (6): traditional versus nontraditional marriage types;
- Domestic Responsibility (3): a specific aspect of traditional marriage;
- Satisfaction (3): personal satisfaction in merging both roles;
- Self-Image (4): effect of career on self-image as wife and mother;
- Career Salience (8): relative importance of career and mother-wife roles; and
- Career Line (7): perception of career involvement.

Responses are on a five-point scale, from "strongly disagree" to "strongly agree."

Sample

The reliability and final item selection were made from the responses of 45 professional women married at least eight years. They were attorneys, college professors, and physicians. Age, geographical, racial, and religious affiliation data are not available.

Reliability

The internal consistency of the scales is very low, as would be expected of such short scales. Only the four-item Self-Image scale (r = .73) and the seven-item Career Line scale (r = .76) reported reliabilities over .70. Other estimates of internal consistency were: Marriage Type, r = .67; Domestic Responsibility, r = .42; Satisfaction, r = .50; and Career Salience, r = .57.

No data concerning stability over time are reported.

Validity

Except for face validity, no validity scores are reported. No factor analysis was attempted to demonstrate whether the six intuitively derived scores are indeed distinct.

Administration

The Dual Career Family Scales is a six-part, paper-and-pencil inventory administered to wives in about 15 minutes.

Location

Pendleton, B. F., Poloma, M. M., & Garland, T. N. (1980). Scales for the investigation of the dual-career family. *Journal of Marriage and the Family*, *42*, 269–275.

Discussion

Notice that the sample for this item is composed of a unique group. All the women had been married at least eight years. Doctors, lawyers, and professors are wealthier, better educated, and more independent than the vast majority of professional women. Teachers, social workers, journalists, bookkeepers, and nurses would have comprised a more frequently encountered group.

The items are too wordy. Perhaps the lawyers and professors in the sample were overly familiar with 37-word questions.

If, as the authors admit, Domestic Responsibility is essentially a subscale of Marriage Type (Traditional), why didn't they combine the two scales to produce a single nine-item scale with a reliability of over .70 rather than use two short scales with lower reliability?

The scales should have been factor analyzed to see if the intuitive division into six scales was justified.

The reality of dual-career marriages makes one applaud any effort to bring research in this area beyond the intelligent guess. This instrument is intended for researchers rather than clinicians, but even for researchers there is a need for caution for scales developed with a unique population. For clinicians, the placement of the questions in order of agreement might provide useful information.

Dual-Career Family Scales

Marriage Type

1. If a child were ill and needed to remain home from school, I would be (have been) more likely to stay home with him/her than my husband.
2. Given the structure of our society, it is important that the woman assume primary responsibility for child care.
3. I consider my husband to be the main breadwinner in the family.
4. My income is as vital to the well-being of our family as is my husband's.
5. I would not work if my husband did not approve.
6. I would not attend a professional convention if it inconvenienced my husband.

Domestic Responsibility

7. Although my husband may assist me, the responsibility for homemaking tasks is primarily mine.
8. If a wife and mother feels she is not meeting her domestic responsibilities due to her career involvement, she should cut back her career demands.
9. I bend over backwards not to have to make demands on my husband that his colleagues (with nonemployed wives) do not have to meet.

Satisfaction

10. I would be a less fulfilled person without my experience of family life.
11. If I had it to do over again, I would not have had any children.
12. If I had it to do over again, I would not have trained for my particular profession.

Self-Image

13. My career has made me a better wife than I would have been otherwise.
14. Married professional women have the best of two worlds: professional employment combined with a full family life.
15. My career has made me a better mother than I otherwise would have been.
16. I spend (spent) as much or more actual time with my children as my non-working neighbors who are active in community affairs.

(*continued*)

The Dual-Career Family Scales (*continued*)

Career Salience

17. I view my work more as a job that I enjoy than as a career.
18. I have cut back on my career involvement in order not to threaten my marriage.
19. My career is as important to my husband as it is to me.
20. I am as career-oriented as my male colleagues.
21. I would recommend that any young woman contemplating a career complete her professional training before marriage.
22. In case of conflicting demands, a professional woman's primary responsibilities are to her husband and children.
23. It is possible for a husband and wife to work in separate cities to maximize career possibilities and have a successful marriage at the same time.
24. If I were to receive an exceptional job offer in another city (one that I wanted to accept), I would not expect my husband to accompany me unless he were sure of a suitable position for himself.

Career Line

25. A married woman's career history should be considered in light of the two sets of demands she faces as a wife and as a professional.
26. Most single career women have greater opportunities to succeed in a profession than do married career women.
27. A married woman's career goals tend to be more modest than those of her male colleagues.
28. I have cut back on my career involvement in order to meet the needs of my family.
29. My career has suffered due to the responsibilities I have (had) as a mother.
30. It is impossible in our present society to combine a career, in the fullest sense of the term (uninterrupted, full-time work with a high degree of commitment and desire for success) with the demands of a family.
31. I consider myself a working woman (have professional employment) rather than a career woman (to whom advancement and exceptional achievement in a profession are important).

21 | MARITAL INSTABILITY SCALE

Alan Booth and John Edwards

Introduction

The Marital Instability Scale was developed to help assess instability among intact couples. In the past, marital instability has been used interchangeably with such other concepts as marital dissolution, divorce, and low marital quality. Although these are related, low marital quality does not necessarily signify a high propensity towards divorce. There are many low quality marriages that remain intact while marriages of higher quality are dissolved.

Description

The Marital Instability Scale was constructed from a pool of 40 cognitive and behavioral items. They included the following aspects of instability: thinking about divorce; talking to the spouse about getting a job, going to school, and so on, without mentioning divorce; talking with the spouse about divorce; talking with significant others about divorce; meeting with clergy or professional counselors about the possibility of divorce; and physically separating from the spouse.

Elimination of inappropriate items, combination of different time periods, and factor analysis helped in the selection of 20 items. These were then related to years married, a social desirability response-tendency scale, education, race, rural–urban residence, wife's employment, and marital happiness. Two items that were found to be inconsistent with these variables were eliminated.

Questions regarding a number of activities and attitudes were combined into single variables. "Never" was coded 0; "ever," 1; "within the last three years," 2; and "now," 3. For the other items a simple "yes," "no," or "don't know" response is required.

The authors also included a compact scale for researchers who find the entire scale impractical. This scale is composed of five questions selected from the inventory. The short form naturally is less reliable than the longer scale.

Sample

The sample contained 2,034 married men and women under the age of 55 who were interviewed by telephone in the fall of 1980. The interviews were conducted as part of a larger study concerning the effects of female labor force participation on marital instability. The sample was compared with estimates made by the U.S. Census and was found to be highly representative of young and middle-aged married persons in the United States.

Reliability

The Marital Instability Scale has a high reliability coefficient, .93. The smaller scale is considerably less reliable; its five-item scale is .75.

Validity

Two sources were used to show that the Marital Instability Scale is valid. First, 36 judges ranked the items, and the mean ratings assigned that item were then correlated to the mean ratings of the total scale by the survey respondents. The correlation was .80. Thus, items that the judges reported as serious with respect to divorce also had high scores on the Marital Instability Scale.

Second, the Marital Instability Scale was also related to a variety of other variables which had been shown to predict divorce and separation in previous research. These included race, religion, residence, female employment, and parental marital dissolution. The Marital Instability Scale significantly correlated with these variables.

Blacks (compared to whites), those who lack religious affiliation (compared to members of major religious bodies), city dwellers (compared to farmers), working women (compared to nonworking women), and children of divorced parents (compared to children of nondivorced parents) received higher scores.

Administration

This is a paper-and-pencil test with a short administration time.

Location

Booth, A., & Edwards, J. (1983). Measuring marital instability. *Journal of Marriage and the Family, 45*, 387–393.

Discussion

The Marital Instability Scale is a reliable and valid predictor of disruption in a marriage and of divorce. If a couple responds "now" to many of the items on the index, successful therapy is unlikely and divorce counseling is called for. This information is sometimes difficult to obtain by simple direct interview. If the goal of therapy requires an optimistic atmosphere, this instrument may be inappropriate.

Marital Instability Scale

Items	Never	Ever	Within Last 3 Years	Now
I have thought marriage in trouble	0	1	2	3
I have talked to others about marital problems	0	1	2	3
I have talked to friends about marital problems	0	1	2	3
Spouse has talked to others about marital problems	0	1	2	3
Spouse has thought marriage in trouble	0	1	2	3
I have thought about divorce	0	1	2	3
Spouse has thought about divorce	0	1	2	3
Either spouse or I have seriously suggested divorce	0	1	2	3
I favor divorce	0	1	2	3
Spouse favors divorce	0	1	2	3
I have initiated conversation about divorce	0	1	2	3
I favor divorce more than spouse	0	1	2	3
Discussed consulting or consulted an attorney	0	1	2	3
Discussed division of property	0	1	2	3
Discussed problems of living apart	0	1	2	3
Discussed filing or actually filed a petition	0	1	2	3
Discussed divorce with family member who approves	0	1	2	3
Discussed divorce with friend who approves	0	1	2	3
Couple has experienced separation	0	1	2	3

Short Marital Instability Scale

Items	Never	Ever	Within Last 3 Years	Now
1. Have you or your husband/wife ever seriously suggested the idea of divorce within the last three years?	0	1	2	3
2. Have you discussed divorce or separation with a close friend?	0	1	2	3
3. Even people who get along quite well with their spouse sometimes wonder whether their marriage is working out. Have you ever thought your marriage might be in trouble?	0	1	2	3
4. Did you talk about consulting an attorney?	0	1	2	3
5. Has the thought of getting a divorce or separation crossed your mind in the past three years?	0	1	2	3

22 | CONFLICT TACTICS SCALES

Murray A. Straus

Introduction

The Conflict Tactics Scales (CTS) were designed to directly measure the reasoning, symbolic aggression, and violence used during family conflicts. The underlying assumption of the test is the belief that it is not the existence of conflict that causes trouble, but rather, inadequate or unsatisfactory modes of resolving conflict.

Description

The CTS were developed on the theory that conflict is an inevitable part of all human association. Without conflict, families, like any other social unit, will stagnate or fail to adapt. On the other hand, high levels of conflict create stress and adversely affect family welfare. It would be consistent with research and catharsis theory for family therapists to stress reasonable ways to deal with conflict rather than help families avoid it.

Three tactics are measured by CTS Form N: the Reasoning scale uses three items; the Symbolic Aggression scale (which Straus usually calls Verbal Aggression, although nonverbal behaviors are included) uses six items; and the Violence scale uses eight items. Each item is scored by giving a 0 for "never in the past year," 1 for "once," 2 for "twice," 3 for "3 to 5 times," 4 for "6 to 10 times," 5 for "11 to 20 times," and 6 for "more than 20 times." Thus the maximum score for the Reasoning scale is 18, for the Symbolic Aggression scale is 36, and for the Violence scale is 48. The scales can be given to measure conflict tactics used with spouse, child, parent, or sibling. Charts can convert raw scores for partners, couples, and parents into percentiles. Weighted scores and percentage methods of computing scores are available, but percentile equivalents for such methods are not reported. The language of the CTS can be understood by children with the possible exception of the words "sulked," "stomped," "spite," and "dispute."

Sample

Surveys were returned in 1976 from a nationally representative sample of 2,143 couples and 899 children who rated their siblings. The completion rate for the survey was 65%, slightly lower than the typical rates of return that mass surveys like this currently obtain.

Reliability

As expected, the longer the scale, the more internally consistent. The internal consistency reliability coefficients for individuals for the three-item Form N Reasoning scale ranged from .50 to .69, for the six-item Symbolic Aggression scale from .77 to .80, and for the eight-item Violence scale from .62 to .83.

Validity

Of 110 college sociology students available, 105 volunteered to take the CTS. Their parents were also tested and 72% responded. There were significant correlations between students' reports and their parents' CTS scores for both Symbolic Aggression (r = .43 to .51) and Violence (r = .33 to .64) but not between students' reports and their parents' Reasoning scores, perhaps because aggression is more dramatic and better remembered.

As theory predicts, Violence scores are positively correlated with parental Violence scores and negatively correlated with socioeconomic class (that is, the poorer couples have higher Violence scores). Husbands with lower prestige and economic resources than their wives have higher Violence scores. Extremely husband-dominant families or (especially) extremely wife-dominant families have significantly higher Violence scores.

Administration

The CTS comprises an orally administered inventory that takes some time to complete but can be quickly scored. The vocabulary is simple enough for most older children and adults. It is recommended that the instructions be read aloud by the researcher or therapist. However, since the norms were established on a sample of people who read to themselves, this scale can be self-administered if written instructions are appropriate.

Location

Straus, M. A. (1979). Measuring intrafamily conflict and violence: The Conflict Tactics (CT) Scales. *Journal of Marriage and the Family, 41*, 75–85.

Discussion

The CTS directly measures the way spouses express anger and handle conflict. The test is short enough (19 items) to require little time, but unfortunately that means that one important scale, the Reasoning scale, lacks internal consistency. Thus, the importance of reasoning as violence control is not properly measured. The percentile chart enables the therapist to compare the couple to a representative cross-section of the population.

Certain items have different meanings for the sexes. When a husband seeks "someone to help settle things" (a therapist?), this is perceived by the wife as "Reasoning." When the wife seeks "someone to help settle things," this is perceived by the husband as "Symbolic Aggression." The use of a knife or a gun is perceived by the wife, but not by the husband, as a unique act.

One item, "crying," was included in the scales to increase face validity but, for some reason, was not used in establishing norms. The author's use of the term Verbal Aggression instead of Symbolic Aggression may reflect how the scales started but does not adequately describe the present scales.

The CTS can be of assistance to the family therapist who wishes to measure the family's history of violence or to evaluate a family for child abuse or spouse abuse.

Husband-Wife Page of CTS Form *N*

No matter how well a couple gets along, there are times when they disagree on major decisions, get annoyed about something the other person does, or just have spats or fights because they're in a bad mood or tired or for some other reason. They also use many different ways of trying to settle their differences. I'm going to read a list of some things that you and your (husband/partner) might have done when you had a dispute, and would first like you to tell me for each one how often you did it in the past year.

Hand Respondent Card A

	First Questions *I Have In Past Year*								*Second Questions* *Husband/Partner In Past Year*								*Follow Up Ever Happened*		
	Never	Once	Twice	3–5 Times	6–10 Times	11–20 Times	More than 20 Times	Don't Know	Never	Once	Twice	3–5 Times	6–10 Times	11–20 Times	More than 20 Times	Don't Know	Yes	No	Don't Know
a. Discussed the issue calmly	0	1	2	3	4	5	6	X	0	1	2	3	4	5	6	X	1	2	X
b. Got information to back up (your/his) side of things	0	1	2	3	4	5	6	X	0	1	2	3	4	5	6	X	1	2	X
c. Brought in or tried to bring in someone to help settle things	0	1	2	3	4	5	6	X	0	1	2	3	4	5	6	X	1	2	X

d. Insulted or swore at the other one	0	1	2	3	4	5	6	X	0	1	2	3	4	5	6	X	1	2	X
e. Sulked and/or refused to talk about it	0	1	2	3	4	5	6	X	0	1	2	3	4	5	6	X	1	2	X
f. Stomped out of the room or house (or yard)	0	1	2	3	4	5	6	X	0	1	2	3	4	5	6	X	1	2	X
*g. Cried	0	1	2	3	4	5	6	X	0	1	2	3	4	5	6	X	1	2	X
h. Did or said something to spite the other one	0	1	2	3	4	5	6	X	0	1	2	3	4	5	6	X	1	2	X
i. Threatened to hit or throw something at the other one	0	1	2	3	4	5	6	X	0	1	2	3	4	5	6	X	1	2	X
j. Threw or smashed or hit or kicked something	0	1	2	3	4	5	6	X	0	1	2	3	4	5	6	X	1	2	X
k. Threw something at the other one	0	1	2	3	4	5	6	X	0	1	2	3	4	5	6	X	1	2	X
l. Pushed, grabbed, or shoved the other one	0	1	2	3	4	5	6	X	0	1	2	3	4	5	6	X	1	2	X
m. Slapped the other one	0	1	2	3	4	5	6	X	0	1	2	3	4	5	6	X	1	2	X
n. Kicked, bit, or hit with a fist	0	1	2	3	4	5	6	X	0	1	2	3	4	5	6	X	1	2	X
o. Hit or tried to hit with something	0	1	2	3	4	5	6	X	0	1	2	3	4	5	6	X	1	2	X
p. Beat up the other one	0	1	2	3	4	5	6	X	0	1	2	3	4	5	6	X	1	2	X
q. Threatened with a knife or gun	0	1	2	3	4	5	6	X	0	1	2	3	4	5	6	X	1	2	X
r. Used a knife or gun	0	1	2	3	4	5	6	X	0	1	2	3	4	5	6	X	1	2	X
*s. Other (PROBE):	0	1	2	3	4	5	6	X	0	1	2	3	4	5	6	X	1	2	X

Second Question Introduction: And what about your (husband/partner)? Tell me how often he (ITEM) in the past year.

For each item circled either "Never" or "Don't Know" for BOTH respondent and partner, ask: Did you or your (husband/partner) ever (ITEM)?

*Items G and S were not used to compute percentile norms.

23 | INTERPERSONAL BEHAVIOR SURVEY

Paul Mauger and David Adkinson

Introduction

Assertive and aggressive behaviors are independent responses. As defined in this instrument assertiveness is behavior-directed towards reaching some desired goal. The client continues in the direction of that goal in spite of obstacles in the environment or the opposition of others. The attitude of the assertive person is positive towards other people. If others do not attempt to block the attainment of a goal, the assertive person's actions are solely aimed at getting rid of the interference and not at attacking the offending individual.

Aggressive behavior originates from attitudes and feelings of hostility towards others. The purpose of aggressive behavior is to attack other individuals or to exert power over them in some fashion. It discourages cooperation. Aggressive behavior is only incidentally directed towards some instrumental goal and often the attainment of that supposed goal is merely a rationalization for the aggressive actions. Aggressive people may deliberately wish to violate the rights of others in pursuing their own goals.

Description

The IBS is a 272-item inventory that differentiates subclasses of assertive and aggressive behaviors rather than just providing single global scores for each of the behaviors. It identifies more specifically behavioral deficits and excesses and can be of help in planning individual interventions.

The IBS contains three sections. Part I has 38 items; Part II has 95 items; Part III has 139 items. Each part contains items with a variety of aggressive and assertive items. Part I alone is intended for a 10-minute or less screening test. Parts I and II together constitute the Short Test. All 272 items of the survey constitute the Long Test.

The individual IBS scales fall under four categories:

1. Validity scales
2. Aggressiveness scales
3. Assertiveness scales
4. Relationship scales

These four categories make up the four sections of the profile. There are three Validity scales:

1. The Denial Scale (similar to the Minnesota Multiphasic Inventory Lie Scale)
2. The Infrequency Scale
3. The Impression Management Scale (similar to the California Personality Inventory's Good Impression Scale)

There are nine Aggressiveness scales:

1. The General Aggressiveness, Rational Scale
2. The General Aggressiveness, Rational-Short Scale
3. The General Aggressiveness, Empirical Scale
4. The Hostile Stance Scale
5. The Expression of Anger Scale
6. The Disregard for Rights Scale
7. The Verbal Aggressiveness Scale
8. The Physical Aggressiveness Scale
9. The Passive Aggressiveness Scale

There are 10 Assertiveness scales:

1. The General Assertiveness, Rational Scale
2. The General Assertiveness, Rational-Short Scale
3. The General Assertiveness, Empirical Scale

4. The Self-Confidence Scale
5. The Initiating Assertiveness Scale
6. The Defending Assertiveness Scale
7. The Frankness Scale
8. The Praise Scale
9. The Requesting Help Scale
10. The Refusing Demands Scale

There are three Relationship scales:

1. Conflict Avoidance Scale
2. The Dependency Scale
3. The Shyness Scale

Sample

The sample used for establishing norms included 21% black, 18% rural. The remainder were primarily urban whites. All 400 males and 400 females came from the South.

Reliability

There are from as few as four to as many as 55 items per scale. The internal consistency reliability varies from .11 to .90 with a median of .69. The test–retest reliability for a 10-week interval varies from .81 to .93 with a median of .90.

Validity

The IBS items possess a certain manifest attractiveness. Factor analysis demonstrated that there are three factors: aggressiveness, assertiveness, and the infrequent response scale.

Assertiveness scores correlate with other tests that measure dominance and do not correlate with other tests that measure hostility and aggression. The aggression scores do correlate with other tests that measure aggression.

Fundamentalists and Veterans Administration psychiatric patients score low in assertiveness. Lacrosse players, assaultive prisoners, sons of U.S. Air Force personnel, and high school students score high in aggressiveness. These findings are consistent with the best guesses of how assertiveness and aggressiveness are found in our population.

Administration

The IBS is a paper-and-pencil test, which requires 10 minutes for the Screening Test, 20 minutes for administration of the Short Test, and 45 minutes for administration of the 272-item Long Test. Answer sheets are very tightly spaced and some clients may need to answer on the question booklets. This would give the therapist the "fun" of recopying the responses before grading them with plastic overlay answer keys. All items are answered true or false.

Location

Mauger, P., & Adkinson, D. (1980). *Interpersonal Behavior Survey manual.* Los Angeles, CA: Western Psychological Services.

Discussion

Studies using the IBS have found that young, low-socioeconomic black males score high on physical aggressiveness. Middle-socioeconomic males are the most assertive. Low-socioeconomic females are the least assertive. Older individuals score higher on the Denial scale and the Praise scale and lower on the Aggressiveness scales. Separate charts are not available for each age group, sex, race, or socioeconomic class. Therefore, counselors should read the manual's section on research results before interpreting the inventory and bear in mind group patterns of answering these kinds of questions.

The IBS can be useful for therapists to detect problems with assertive or aggressive behaviors in treatment planning and outcome evaluation. Caution should be taken not to exaggerate subscale score differences since short subscales are not reliable.

Literature is available on use of the IBS with couples (Hebblewhite, 1979; Mouzon, 1980). The IBS is suited for use with couples, since many of the marital issues that are dealt with in therapy arise from inappropriate methods of conflict resolution. The IBS can be used to detect differences in the interpersonal styles of husbands and wives. The discovery of these areas of difference can help the marriage therapist interpret couples' complaints in the context of their typical patterns of interaction. The distinction between assertion and aggression is basic.

IBS can be purchased from: Western Psychological Services, 12031 Wilshire Boulevard, Los Angeles, CA 90025.

REFERENCES

Hebblewhite, M. (1979). Assertiveness and aggressiveness of spouses as variables in couple adjustment. Unpublished Master's Thesis, Georgia State University.

Mouzon, R. (1980). Assertiveness and aggressiveness and its relationship to marital adjustment in black couples. Unpublished Master's thesis, Georgia State University.

Sample Items from the IBS

Denial Scale

11.* Sometimes I blame others when things go wrong.

Infrequency Scale

30. I enjoy making people angry.

Impression Management

125. I rarely tease others.

General Aggressiveness, Rational

4. I rarely lose my temper.

General Aggressiveness, Empirical

14. I try not to give people a hard time.

Hostile Stance

32. There are times when I would enjoy hurting people I love.

Expression of Anger

19. I get mad easily.

Disregard of Rights

53. Sometimes you can't help hurting others to get ahead.

Verbal Aggressiveness

50. I usually tell people off when they disagree with me.

Physical Aggressiveness

61. I would not hit back if a friend hit me first.

Passive Aggressiveness

180. Others seldom have to remind me to finish things I have started.

General Assertiveness, Rational

108. If someone were annoying me during a movie, I would ask that person to stop.

General Assertiveness, Empirical

21. I get embarrassed easily.

Self-Confidence

94. Rather than ask for a favor I will do without.

Initiating Assertiveness

75. In most situations I would rather listen than talk.

Defending Assertiveness

89. I find it difficult to stand up for my rights.

Frankness

7. It is very important to me to be able to speak my mind.

Praise

40. I find it difficult to compliment or praise others.

Requesting Help

115. I find it difficult to ask a friend for a favor.

Refusing Demands

85. I find it difficult to say "no" to a salesperson.

Conflict Avoidance

97. I enjoy being involved in a good argument.

Dependency

151. I usually feel insecure unless I am near someone on whose support I can depend.

Shyness

241. I often dread going into a room by myself when others are already gathered and talking.

*Numbers indicate actual number of sample item on the IBS.

24 | FAMILY THERAPIST RATING SCALE

Fred Piercy, Roger Laird, and Zain Mohammed

Introduction

Writers in the field of family therapy have for some time advocated opening the therapy session to observation and active supervision. The Family Therapist Rating Scale was developed to enable observers to quantify and compare therapist skills.

Description

A pool of 375 items was selected that reflected goal-directed therapist activities believed necessary by therapists from diverse theoretical orientations. Duplicate and lengthy items were eliminated. Three doctoral-level therapists placed the activities in five categories suggested by Levant (1980) and eliminated items considered unimportant. Seventy-one items were retained.

Ten doctoral students with at least two years' experience as family therapists then rated 142 videotaped two-minute vignettes by an actor/therapist which illustrated each specific skill. Ten items in each of five categories were chosen for their ability to best discriminate between effective and ineffective behavior with the greatest degree of agreement by the 10 doctoral students.

The five categories of therapeutic behaviors are: Structuring (defines needs, clarifies expectation, etc.); Relationship (engenders hope, empathy, improves members self-esteem, etc.); Historical (explores mate selection, collects information about origin of problem, etc.); Structural/Process (helps establish boundaries, observes, then intervenes, etc.); and Experiential (uses role playing, sculpting, fantasy sharing, etc.)

Each behavior is rated on a seven-point scale: "not present" (0); "ineffective" (1); "neutral" (2); "minimally effective" (3); "effective" (4); "very effective" (5); and "maximally effective" (6). On each scale a therapist can thus score between 0 and 60.

Sample

One experienced family therapist rated the performances of 29 graduate family therapy students at East Texas State University counseling a coached family. Their performance was correlated with the ranking of these students by their respective doctoral-level supervisors. Twenty-five graduate therapy students and 19 experienced therapists were rated by the same rater while they counseled a coached family group. These 44 therapists were asked to categorize their own technique according to the five categories used.

Reliability

The interrater reliability for the original two-minute videotape vignettes varied between .61 and .87. Doctoral students seemed to agree, for the most part, about what they saw. The internal consistency reliability estimates for the 44 therapists by the expert rater varied between a .72 for Historical behavior to a high .95 for Relationship behavior. For this one rater, at least, consistent scores were sometimes available.

Validity

The correlation between supervisor ratings and scale ratings were significantly above chance on three of the scales: Relationship, rho = .43; Structural/Process, rho = .37; and Experiential, rho = .42.

The experienced family therapists scored significantly higher on each of the five scales than inexperienced family therapists.

Each of the 44 therapists was more likely than chance to be rated most effective in his or her preferred category.

The selection of the initial 71 items by three independent judges constitutes expert judgment of the choice of items (face validity) on the scales.

Administration

The minimum time needed to administer this scale is not specified. It is helpful to read the article by Levant (1980) prior to using the scale.

Location

Piercy, F., Laird, R., & Mohammed, Z. (1983). A Family Therapist Rating Scale. *Journal of Marital and Family Therapy, 9*, 49-59.

Discussion

There is an unquestioned need for a rating scale that does not require the immense amount of time now required by suggested interaction analysis techniques that are being developed. The Family Therapist Rating Scale requires the rater to attend to only a limited number of family therapist skills and does not require the rater to code or note every verbal utterance.

The fact that much of the reliability and validity data are based on the evaluations of one experienced family therapist should lead the therapist educator to be cautious. The scale deliberately uses global ratings in its final form and these are most susceptible to halo effect. The scale starts with assumptions about what constitutes good marital therapy, an approach which (as the authors themselves justly note) groups extremely different schools under the same measuring approach. But the scale, even as presently constructed, is simple enough and sound enough to justify its use in supervision and training as well as in research.

REFERENCE

Levant, R. (1980). Classification of the field of family therapy: A review of prior attempts and a new paradigmatic model. *American Journal of Family Therapy, 8*, 3-16.

Family Therapist Rating Scale

Directions: Rate the relative effectiveness with which the family therapist engaged in the behaviors listed below. Some of these behaviors may be associated with a school of therapy other than your own. Try to be neutral and rate the relative effectiveness with which the therapist performs each behavior regardless of whether you agree or disagree with the type of intervention. In other words, try not to rate the model of therapy, just the behavior as identified by the statement on the rating scale.

Not Present (0); Ineffective (1); Neutral (2); Minimally Effective (3); Effective (4); Very Effective (5); Maximally Effective (6)

0 1 2 3 4 5 6

Structuring Behaviors

1. ___ : ___ : ___ : ___ : ___ : ___ : ___ : Helps the family define their needs.
2. ___ : ___ : ___ : ___ : ___ : ___ : ___ : Stops chaotic interchanges.
3. ___ : ___ : ___ : ___ : ___ : ___ : ___ : Shifts approach when one way of gathering information is not working.
4. ___ : ___ : ___ : ___ : ___ : ___ : ___ : Uses short, specific and clear communications.
5. ___ : ___ : ___ : ___ : ___ : ___ : ___ : Asks open-ended questions.
6. ___ : ___ : ___ : ___ : ___ : ___ : ___ : Helps clients rephrase "why" questions into statements.
7. ___ : ___ : ___ : ___ : ___ : ___ : ___ : Makes a brief introductory statement about the purpose of the interview.
8. ___ : ___ : ___ : ___ : ___ : ___ : ___ : Lays down ground rules for therapeutic process.
9. ___ : ___ : ___ : ___ : ___ : ___ : ___ : Clarifies own and client's expectations of therapy.
10. ___ : ___ : ___ : ___ : ___ : ___ : ___ : Explicitly structures or directs interaction among family members.

Relationship Behaviors

1. ___ : ___ : ___ : ___ : ___ : ___ : ___ : Engenders hope.
2. ___ : ___ : ___ : ___ : ___ : ___ : ___ : Uses self-disclosure.
3. ___ : ___ : ___ : ___ : ___ : ___ : ___ : Demonstrates warmth.
4. ___ : ___ : ___ : ___ : ___ : ___ : ___ : "Communicates" the attitude that the client's problem is of real importance.
5. ___ : ___ : ___ : ___ : ___ : ___ : ___ : Tone of voice conveys sensitivity to the client's feelings.
6. ___ : ___ : ___ : ___ : ___ : ___ : ___ : Speaks at a comfortable pace.
7. ___ : ___ : ___ : ___ : ___ : ___ : ___ : Empathizes with family members.
8. ___ : ___ : ___ : ___ : ___ : ___ : ___ : Confirms family members' experience of an event.
9. ___ : ___ : ___ : ___ : ___ : ___ : ___ : Attempts to improve the self-esteem of individual family members.
10. ___ : ___ : ___ : ___ : ___ : ___ : ___ : Demonstrates a good sense of humor.

Historical Behaviors

1. ___ : ___ : ___ : ___ : ___ : ___ : ___ : Directly asks about the current relationship between a spouse and his/her parents and siblings.
2. ___ : ___ : ___ : ___ : ___ : ___ : ___ : Explores the couple's mate selection process.
3. ___ : ___ : ___ : ___ : ___ : ___ : ___ : Emphasizes cognitions.

(*continued*)

Family Therapist Rating Scale (*continued*)

	0	1	2	3	4	5	6	
4.	___	___	___	___	___	___	___	Assembles a detailed family history.
5.	___	___	___	___	___	___	___	Avoids becoming triangulated by the family.
6.	___	___	___	___	___	___	___	Attempts to help clients directly deal with parents and adult siblings about previously avoided issues.
7.	___	___	___	___	___	___	___	Assigns or suggests that family members visit extended family members.
8.	___	___	___	___	___	___	___	Maintains an objective stance.
9.	___	___	___	___	___	___	___	Makes interpretations.
10.	___	___	___	___	___	___	___	Collects detailed information about the etiology of the identified problem.

Structural/Process Behaviors

1.	___	___	___	___	___	___	___	Checks out pronouns to see who did what to whom.
2.	___	___	___	___	___	___	___	Assigns tasks both within the session and outside it.
3.	___	___	___	___	___	___	___	Concentrates on the interaction of the system rather than the intrapsychic dynamics.
4.	___	___	___	___	___	___	___	Employs paradoxical intention.
5.	___	___	___	___	___	___	___	Relabels family symptoms.
6.	___	___	___	___	___	___	___	Reorders behavioral sequences (e.g., order of speaking, who speaks to whom).
7.	___	___	___	___	___	___	___	Rearranges the physical seating of family members.
8.	___	___	___	___	___	___	___	Helps the family establish appropriate boundaries.
9.	___	___	___	___	___	___	___	Elicits covert family conflicts, alliances and coalitions.
10.	___	___	___	___	___	___	___	Assumes the role of expert technician who observes and then intervenes.

Experiential Behaviors

1.	___	___	___	___	___	___	___	Uses family sculpting.
2.	___	___	___	___	___	___	___	Encourages family members to find their own solutions.
3.	___	___	___	___	___	___	___	Encourages individuals to share their fantasies.
4.	___	___	___	___	___	___	___	Asks for current feelings.
5.	___	___	___	___	___	___	___	Lets the clients choose the subject of the session.
6.	___	___	___	___	___	___	___	Attempts to focus on process rather than content.
7.	___	___	___	___	___	___	___	Uses role playing.
8.	___	___	___	___	___	___	___	Responds to his/her own discomfort.
9.	___	___	___	___	___	___	___	Uses own affect to elicit affect in family members.
10.	___	___	___	___	___	___	___	Keeps the interaction in the here and now.

Family Therapist Rating Scale Profile

Therapist's Name ______________________ Comments ______________________________
Date ______________________________ ______________________________________
Rater ______________________________ ______________________________________

Mean Rating of Behaviors Observed	Raw Score	Structuring	Relationship	Historical	Structural/ Process	Experiential
6	60	-	-	-	-	-
	55	-	-	-	-	-
5	50	-	-	-	-	-
	45	-	-	-	-	-
4	40	-	-	-	-	-
	35	-	-	-	-	-
3	30	-	-	-	-	-
	25	-	-	-	-	-
2	20	-	-	-	-	-
	15	-	-	-	-	-
1	10	-	-	-	-	-
	5	-	-	-	-	-

Note: A profile of a family therapist's behavior may be constructed in two ways. In one approach, raw scores, the total points within each category, may be added and placed on the profile. However, it may at times be helpful to use the mean ratings of only those behaviors actually observed within each category. The above profile has been constructed to accommodate either method.

7

Minnesota Family Inventories

INTRODUCTION

The University of Minnesota has long been a center for the construction of many personality and interest inventories. The Minnesota Multiphasic Inventory is even more widely used today (thanks to the computer) than it was when it was first published. The leading vocational scale, the Strong-Campbell Interest Inventory, is also a product of the Minnesota School. It is not surprising then that this group should have produced many useful family inventories.

The Minnesota School developed a comprehensive series of inventories designed or revised for use in a national survey of 1,140 couples and 412 adolescents from 31 states. The sample represented all stages of the family life cycle: 121 young couples without children, 148 families with preschoolers, 129 families with school-age children (ages six to 12), 261 families with adolescents (13 to 18), 191 launching families (where the oldest child is at least 19), 144 empty-nest families, and 146 retired couples (male over 65). These families were surveyed in January 1982.

It is important to note that the comparison group is almost all white Lutherans. Religious commitment and lifestyle could affect responses, especially to the "satisfied with religion" questions on the Family of Life Scale. The size, age, and geographic dispersal of the sample is appealing. The specific religious persuasion of the sample must be remembered before interpreting.

FACES III is the third revision of the Family Adaptability and Cohesion Scales by Olson, Portner, and Lavee (see Measure #25). Parent and adolescent responses can be charted on four levels of adaptability (chaotic, flexible, structured, and rigid) and four levels of cohesion (disengaged, separated, connected, and enmeshed). The theoretical basis for the inventory is the circumplex model that advocates an Aristotelian-style moderation of "balanced" cohesion and adaptability. Profiles of the father's, mother's, and adolescent's perceived and ideal family can graphically present the level of satisfaction with the current family system. Beavers and Voeller (1983) criticizes the model for ignoring the developmental stage of the family life cycle.

The Quality of Life scale by Olson and Barnes (see Measure #26) has a 40-item Parent Form that measures satisfaction with marriage and family life, friends, extended family, health, home, education, leisure and work time, religion, employment, mass media, financial well-being, and neighborhood and community. A 25-item Adolescent Form measures satisfaction in the same areas except for marriage and employment. The total scale has high reliability and moderately high stability.

Family Strengths by Olson, Larsen, and McCubbin (see Measure #27) is a brief 12-item scale that measures family pride and family sense of competence. Science clarifies art. This scale identifies and measures what Tolstoy called the way "all happy families resemble one another."

FILE, or Family Inventory of Life Events and Changes, by McCubbin, Patterson, and Wilson (see Measure #28) is a 71-item questionnaire based on psychobiological stress research by Holmes and Rahe (1967). Any excessive life change can upset the body's capacity for readjustment and produce stress. These stressors include family conflict and parenting strain, marital strain, pregnancy and childbearing strain, financial and business strain, work and school transition, illness, dependency, losses, and family legal violations. A 50-item variation is available for teenagers. It is sometimes necessary for family members to realize that the crises they have been through affect marital and family satisfaction.

How the family copes with stresses is measured by Family Crisis-Oriented Personal Scale (F-COPES), a 29-item scale by McCubbin, Olson, and Larsen (see Measure #29) appropriate for parents and adolescents. Five different coping mechanisms are measured: active acquiring of support from relatives, friends, neighbors, and extended family; reframing stressful events to make them more manageable; seeking spiritual support; mobilizing family to accept help from counselors, doctors, and community agencies; and passive appraisal.

The PREPARE (Premarital Personal and Relationship Evaluation)-ENRICH (Evaluating and Nurturing Relationship Issues, Communication, and Happiness) Inventories were developed by Fournier, Olson, and Druckman (see Measure #30). They are computer-scored and especially developed for use in premarital counseling and marital weekend retreats. The computer printout highlights potential strength or agreement areas as well as areas of dissatisfaction and disagreement. Areas described by the inventories include personality issues, communication, conflict resolution, financial management, leisure activities, sexual relationship, children and marriage, family and friends, equalitarian roles, and religious orientation. The growth of church and community counseling services for the engaged and recently wed provides a market for these inventories.

Schaefer and Olson's Personal Assessment of Intimacy in Relationships (PAIR) (see Measure #31) measures five kinds of intimacy: emotional, social, sexual, intellectual, and recreational. It surrenders some reliability for the convenience of a very short (36-item) inventory.

The various Minnesota Inventories may be purchased from: Family Social Science, 290 McNeal Hall, University of Minnesota, St. Paul, MN 55108.

REFERENCES

Beavers, W., & Voeller, M. (1983). Family models: Comparing and contrasting the Olson circumplex model with the Beavers' system model. *Family Process, 21*, 250–260.

Holmes, T., & Rahe, R. (1967). The social adjustment scale. *Journal of Psychosomatic Research*, 11, 213–218.

25 | FAMILY ADAPTABILITY AND COHESION EVALUATION SCALES III

David H. Olson, Joyce Portner, and Yoav Lavee

Introduction

Some old-fashioned families would now be characterized as rigidly enmeshed. Their opposite, chaotically disengaged families, are equally subject to criticism by therapists and to ridicule by dramatists. Moderation in adaptability and in cohesion is the underlying theory behind the Family Adaptability and Cohesion Evaluation Scales III (FACES III). FACES III is a 20-item scale that measures the degree of family adaptability and cohesion.

Description

According to Olson, Russell, and Sprenkle (1979), family therapy literature reveals three dimensions of family behavior: adaptability, the extent to which the family system is flexible and subject to change; cohesion, the emotional bonding that family members have towards one another; and communication. There are other measures of family communication; The first FACES was developed to measure family adaptability and cohesion.

In 1979 a 111-item, self-report scale was developed. Tryouts reduced this to 90, then 50, then 30, and finally the present 20 items. Adaptability items measure leadership, discipline, child control, roles, and rules. Cohesion items measure emotional bonding, supportiveness, family boundaries, shared time and friends, and shared activities.

Like Minuchin (1974), this scale speaks of four levels of family cohesion: disengaged, separated, connected, and enmeshed. There are also four levels of family adaptability: chaotic, flexible, structured, and rigid. This creates 16 possible family systems: four balanced on both dimensions, four extreme on both dimensions, and eight mid-range.

The scales are designed to be given twice. One form asks each member to describe the family; the other asks how each member would like the family to be.

Although such terms as "balanced" and "extreme" reveal the authors' biases, the authors concede that extreme types of families may function well as long as all the family members like it that way and *crises do not demand flexible behavior*. A couple's version of the scales is available for couples without children in the home. Items dealing with child control were dropped from the couple's version and items dealing with negotiating were substituted.

Sample

FACES was developed using varying samples. Thirty-five marriage and family counselors assessed its clinical usefulness and 410 young adults (undescribed) also evaluated the test. Then, 210 father-mother-one-adolescent groups were studied.

FACES III was developed using 464 adults with an average age of 30.5 who are otherwise undescribed. They took a 90-item form from whose factor analysis and reliability were estimated. A sample of 124 high school and university students (average age 19.2) were used to study test–retest reliability. The final sample used 2,082 parents from nonproblem families and 416 adolescents from these families. These families ranged from young couples to retired couples, who were primarily Lutheran and white. FACES III seems to have used this same sample.

Reliability

The internal consistency reliability was .77 for the 10-item Cohesion scale, .62 for the 10-item Adaptability scale, and .68 for the total FACES III. These are much lower reliability scores than were reported for the 30-item FACES II.

Test–retest (stability after four to five weeks) reliability scores for the much longer 50-item scale were .83 for Cohesion, .80 for Adaptability, and .84 for the total scale. Test–retest reliability scores for FACES III are not available.

Validity

Factor analysis helped select the final 20 items. Adaptability and Cohesion on FACES II were so highly related that they could not really be said to be measuring different dimensions of family structure. FACES III has dramatically increased the independence of these two subscales—so much so that a *total* score may be meaningless. In addition, Adaptability items have been eliminated if they influence individuals to report themselves in too favorable a light. The resultant scale is now named "Adaptability (Change)."

There is no correlation (r = .00) between adaptability (change) and social desirability, yet some correlation remains between cohesion and social desirability (r = .39).

Bell (1982) compared 33 families with runaways with 117 nonproblem families. Significantly, more mothers and adolescents (but not fathers) of the nonproblem families were in the balanced area. Clinic families tended to be more chaotic-disengaged (30%) then nonclinic families (12%).

Rodick, Henggler, and Hanson (1986) evaluated 58 mother-adolescent son dyads from families where the fathers were absent. Half of the sons were juvenile offenders. The other half had no history of arrest or psychiatric referral. Twenty of the normal families and only two of the families with a delinquent son were balanced on both dimensions. When extreme scores were reported by normal families, they tended to be extreme levels of cohesion and change.

Olson (1986) reports consistent findings of lack of balance in chemically dependent, alcoholic, neurotic, schizophrenic, and sex-offender families. No evidence, however, linked the specific symptom with any specific type of family system.

Administration

FACES III is a 20-item, paper-and-pencil scale. Each item has a five-point response option. The scale is first taken with the instruction to family members to "Describe your family now"; then they are asked to respond to, "Ideally, how would you like your family to be?" Discrepancy scores measure the level of satisfaction. The reading level is about seventh grade. Perception and ideal scores of various members can be charted in a family profile for interpretation.

Location

Olson, D. H., Portner, J., & Lavee, Y. (1985). FACES III: Family Adaptability and Cohesion Evaluations Scales. In D. Olson, H. McCubbin, H. Barnes, A. Larsen, M. Muxen, & M. Wilson (Eds.),

Family inventories (revised edition). St. Paul, MN: Family Social Science, University of Minnesota.

Discussion

FACES III is a very popular research instrument. Literally hundreds of studies used FACES in one of its forms. Wives tended to rate Cohesion and Adaptability significantly higher at any stage of the family life cycle than did husbands. Cohesion scores were significantly lower when adolescents were in the family.

"Adaptability" was an unfortunate title. Since adaptability is a positive growth concept, moderate adaptability is no virtue. Recently, Olson and colleagues have retitled their charts "Adaptability (Change)." Change is a much better name; too little or too much change could be properly stigmatized as rigid or chaotic. However, the name FACES has become too well known to surrender, so the misleading word "Adaptability" remains in the title.

One aspect of the Cohesion scale, autonomy, was removed in response to criticism. Autonomy is also a growth concept.

Some studies question whether enmeshed families, as measured by FACES III, are really malfunctioning. Enmeshment is not simply high cohesion. It is the unwillingness or inability to respect individuality and boundaries. Thus, the authors score a strongly negative response to the item, "We approve of each other's friends," as a sign of disengagement. In fact, such a response may indicate enmeshment because of interference in another's friendships.

The use of both a perceived and an ideal score enables the therapist to measure marital satisfaction and to point out discrepancies between perceptions or goals.

There are low (.46) to very low (.13) correlations between family descriptions by various family members. What an adolescent perceives as rigidity might be perceived by the mother as flexibility. Such discrepancies are the subject of therapy. The authors advise giving the forms to as many family members as possible to sense the dynamics of the family system.

FACES III is short, with respectable reliability in the Cohesion scale. It can be given before, during, and after therapy. FACES III can be used to describe families of origin and can make families aware of types of family systems unlike their own. The low reliability level reported for

Adaptability is attributed to "the complexity and richness" (Olson et al., 1985, p. 22) of this dimension. Thus, this scale must be interpreted with some caution.

REFERENCES

Bell, R. (1982). Parent-adolescent relationships in families with a runaway: Interaction types and the circumplex model. Unpublished doctoral dissertation, University of Minnesota, St. Paul, Minnesota.

Minuchin, S. (1974). *Families and family therapy*. Cambridge, MA: Harvard University Press.

Olson, D. (1986). Circumplex model VII: Validation studies and FACES III. *Family Process, 25*, 337-351.

Olson, D., Russell, C. S., & Sprenkle, D. H. (1979). Circumplex model of marital and family systems II: Empirical studies and clinical intervention. In J. Vincent (Ed.), *Advances in family intervention, assessment and theory*. Greenwich, CT: JAI.

Rodick, J., Henggler, S., & Hanson, C. (1986). An evaluation of Family Adaptability and Cohesion Scales (FACES) and the circumplex model. *Journal of Abnormal Child Psychology, 14*, 77-87.

FACES III

DESCRIBE YOUR FAMILY NOW:

_____ 1. Family members ask each other for help.

_____ 2. In solving problems, the children's suggestions are followed.

_____ 3. We approve of each other's friends.

_____ 4. Children have a say in their discipline.

_____ 5. We like to do things with just our immediate family.

_____ 6. Different persons act as leaders in our family.

_____ 7. Family members feel closer to other family members than to people outside the family.

_____ 8. Our family changes its way of handling tasks.

_____ 9. Family members like to spend free time with each other.

_____ 10. Parent(s) and children discuss punishment together.

_____ 11. Family members feel very close to each other.

_____ 12. The children make the decisions in our family.

_____ 13. When our family gets together for activities, everybody is present.

_____ 14. Rules change in our family.

_____ 15. We can easily think of things to do together as a family.

_____ 16. We shift household responsibilities from person to person.

_____ 17. Family members consult other family members on their decisions.

_____ 18. It is hard to identify the leader(s) in our family.

_____ 19. Family togetherness is very important.

_____ 20. It is hard to tell who does which household chores.

FAMILY SOCIAL SCIENCE, 290 McNeal Hall, University of Minnesota, St. Paul, MN 55108

26 | QUALITY OF LIFE

David H. Olson and Howard L. Barnes

Introduction

There are two commonly used ways to measure the quality of life. The first is to measure quantity (income, bathtubs, television sets, air pollution level) and infer quality. The second is to ask. The Quality of Life scale is included among family inventories because when people are asked about their quality of life, the degree of satisfaction with their own families is always included. The Quality of Life scale is a five-response, 40-item scale for parents, 25-item scale for adolescents. It measures satisfaction with family life, friends, extended family, health, home, education, time, religion, mass media, financial well-being, neighborhood and community, and (for parents) employment.

Description

The Quality of Life scale is based on items identified in studies by Campbell, Converse, and Rodgers (1976) and the Minnesota Quality of Life study (Stoekler & Gage, 1978). To these items were added questions concerning health (rather than health care) and reaction to the mass media.

The areas measured by the scale and the number of items for each area (parent scale is underlined; adolescent, not underlined) are:

- Marriage and Family Life (<u>4</u>, 3)
- Friends (<u>1</u>, 1)
- Extended Family (<u>1</u>, 1)
- Health (<u>2</u>, 2)
- Home (<u>5</u>, 2)
- Education (<u>2</u>, 1)
- Free Time (<u>5</u>, 2)
- Religion (<u>2</u>, 2)

- Employment (2, 0)
- Mass Media (4, 4)
- Financial Well-Being (6, 3)
- Neighborhood and Community (6, 4)

Sample

The Campbell study used 2,164 individuals; the Stoeckler and Gage study used 100 families from a metropolitan area and another 100 families from small towns (population 5,000–10,000). Olson and Barnes also used a nationwide sample of over 2,000 white Lutherans. Stability estimates used a sample of 124 Minnesota high school and college students from 12 different classes. The average age in the stability study was 19.2.

Reliability

Internal consistency reliability estimates for the Parent scale were .92 and for the Adolescent scale, from .85 to .87. Internal consistency estimates are not reported for any subscale (perhaps because a few have only one item). The stability estimate for adolescents (after four to five weeks) was an acceptable .65 for the total scale. Individual subscale estimates ranged from .40 for leisure to .72 for family life with a median estimate of .51. Interestingly, the family life subscale stability estimate was the highest; the extended family subscale stability estimate was the second lowest, .44.

Validity

Other than factor analysis, which in general did support the existence of 12 factors, only the manifest content of the items is used to prove validity. Certain items did not fall neatly into the assigned areas: the amount of time family members watch television; the number of children in the family; and both religion questions.

Administration

Quality of Life-Parent Form is a 40-item, five-response scale that takes about five to 15 minutes to complete. The Adolescent Form has 25 items. Computer scoring is available but not required.

Location

Olson, D. H., & Barnes, H. L. (1985). Quality of Life. In D. H. Olson, H. I. McCubbin, H. L. Barnes, A. S. Larsen, M. Muxen, & M. Wilson (Eds.), *Family inventories* (revised edition). St. Paul, MN: Family Social Science, University of Minnesota.

Discussion

The adolescent sample seems to be at an average age of 19.2, about three to four years above the typical age most people think of when they refer to "adolescents." The stability of specific satisfaction subscale scores (except for "your family life") indicates how rapidly these satisfactions—or more accurately these reports of satisfaction—change.

The Quality of Life scale does measure reliably parent and adolescent satisfaction with many aspects of family concern. Several items in the mass media subscale seem irrelevant to family counseling. "The amount of time family members watch TV" is, of course, an important family question. But satisfaction with the quality of television programs, movies, newspapers, and magazines is irrelevant. Unless what is meant is that "My spouse (or child) watches or reads media productions of which I disapprove because they are at best a waste of time." It is no wonder that the only item in this scale that is a family concern has statistically so little in common with the other items.

REFERENCES

Campbell, A., Converse, P., & Rodgers, W. (1976). *The quality of American life: Perceptions, evaluations, and satisfactions*. New York: Russell Sage Foundation.

Stoeckeler, H. S., & Gage, M. G. (1978). *Quality of Life*. Agricultural Experiment Station Miscellaneous Report 154. University of Minnesota.

Quality of Life
Parent Form

HOW SATISIFED ARE YOU WITH:

MARRIAGE AND FAMILY LIFE	1. Your family
	2. Your marriage
	3. Your children
	4. Number of children in your family
FRIENDS	5. Your friends
EXTENDED FAMILY	6. Your relationship with relatives (aunts, uncles, grandparents, etc.)
HEALTH	7. Your own health
	8. Health of other family members
HOME	9. Your current housing arrangement
	10. Your household responsibilites
	11. Other family members' household responsibilities
	12. Space for your own needs
	13. Space for your family needs
EDUCATION	14. The amount of education you have
	15. The educational programs designed to improve marriage and family life
TIME	16. Amount of free time
	17. Time for self
	18. Time for family
	19. Time for housework
	20. Time for earning money
RELIGION	21. The religious life of your family
	22. The religious life in your community
EMPLOYMENT	23. Your principal occupation (job)
	24. Your job security
MASS MEDIA	25. The amount of time family members watch TV
	26. The quality of TV programs
	27. The quality of movies
	28. The quality of newspapers and magazines
FINANCIAL WELLBEING	29. Your level of income
	30. Money for family necessities
	31. Your ability to handle financial emergencies
	32. Amount of money you owe (mortgage, loans, credit cards)
	33. Level of saving
	34. Money for future needs of family
NEIGHBORHOOD AND COMMUNITY	35. The schools in your community
	36. The shopping in your community
	37. The safety in your community
	38. The neighborhood you live in
	39. The recreational facilities (parks, play grounds, programs, etc.)
	40. The health care services

Quality of Life
Adolescent Form

HOW SATISFIED ARE YOU WITH:

Your Family Life
1. Your family
2. Your brothers and sisters
3. Number of children in your family

Friends
4. Your friends

Extended Family
5. Your relationship with relatives (aunts, uncles, grandparents, etc.)

Health
6. Your own health
7. Health of other family members

Home
8. Your current housing arrangements (the place you live)
9. Your respnsibilities around the house

Education
10. Your current school situation

Leisure
11. Amount of free time you have
12. The way you use your free time

Religion
13. The religious life of your family
14. The religious life in your community

Mass Media
15. The amount of time family members watch TV
16. The quality of TV programs
17. The quality of movies
18. The quality of newspapers and magazines

Financial Wellbeing
19. Your family's ability to buy necessities
20. Your family's ability to buy luxuries
21. The amount of money you have to spend

Neighborhood and Community
22. The availability of shopping in your community
23. The safety in your community
24. The neighborhood you live in
25. The recreational facilities (parks, playgrounds, programs, etc.)

University of Minnesota
Family Social Science
290 McNeal Hall
St. Paul, MN 55108

27 | FAMILY STRENGTHS

David H. Olson, Andrea S. Larsen, and Hamilton I. McCubbin

Introduction

The famous opening line of Tolstoy's *Anna Karenina* reads, "All happy families resemble one another, but each unhappy family is unhappy in its own way." That is probably why soap operas and researchers prefer to concentrate on family disorganization. Family Strengths is a brief 12-item, five-point scale that attempts to define the ways in which happy families resemble one another.

Description

Stinnet and Sauer (Stinnet, 1981) questioned families that had been identified as strong. Building on their work, Olson and colleagues (1983) conducted a national survey that helped identify five factors of family strength: love, religion, respect, communication, and individuality. Based on further research, a 25-item list was produced measuring three dimensions: pride (including respect, trust, and loyalty), positive values and beliefs, and accord (the family sense of competence).

A factor analysis reduced the 25 items to 12. A second sample and analysis merged family pride with shared beliefs, and a 12-item inventory emerged: seven items positively scored measure family pride; five items negatively scored measure family accord.

Sample

The factor analysis that produced the Family Strengths scale used students in one course at the University of Minnesota, their families, and their friends. A large percentage were working professionals in the area of human services. Final reliability studies used 2,582 white Lutherans from a national sample.

Reliability

The internal consistency estimates for pride is .88, for accord, .72, and for the total scale, .83. The stability estimates (after four weeks) are .73 for pride, .79 for accord, and .78 for the total scale.

Validity

Factor analysis did discover two separate factors, but it must be noted that perhaps the two factors have nothing to do with their different content but are merely the product of phrasing seven items positively and five negatively. Other than this, the only validity reported is the reasonable content of the items.

Administration

Family Strengths is a 12-item, five-point rating inventory that can be taken in two to five minutes by teenagers or adults. One word that might possibly trouble some 13-year-olds is "confide." There may be some confusion in reverse scoring the five negative accord items.

Location

Olson, D. H., Larsen, A. S., & McCubbin, H. I. (1985). Family Strengths. In D. Olson, H. McCubbin, H. Barnes, A. Larsen, M. Muxen, & M. Wilson (Eds.), *Family inventories* (revised edition). St. Paul, MN: Family Social Science, University of Minnesota.

Discussion

Initially Family Strengths showed more promise than its final version demonstrates. Love, religion, respect, communication, and individuality are five important categories. The final version's pride and accord are comparatively bland. The final product is short enough that individual items—many of which are quite interesting—can serve to stimulate discussion.

REFERENCES

Olson, D., et al. (1983). *Families: What makes them work*. Beverly Hills: Sage.

Stinnet, N. (1981). In search of strong families. In N. Stinnet, B. Chesser, & J. De Frain (Eds.), *Building family strengths: Blueprints for action*. Lincoln, NE: University of Nebraska Press.

Family Strengths

(+) 1. We can express our feelings.

(-) 2. We tend to worry about many things.

(+) 3. We really do trust and confide in each other.

(-) 4. We have the same problems over and over.

(+) 5. Family members feel loyal to the family.

(-) 6. Accomplishing what we want to do seems difficult for us.

(-) 7. We are critical of each other.

(+) 8. We share similar values and beliefs as a family.

(+) 9. Things work out well for us as a family.

(+) 10. Family members respect one another.

(-) 11. There are many conflicts in our family.

(+) 12. We are proud of our family.

28 | FAMILY INVENTORY OF LIFE EVENTS AND CHANGES

Hamilton I. McCubbin, Joan M. Patterson, and Lance R. Wilson

Introduction

One of the key ideas from biology that psychologists appreciate is homeostasis, the tendency of a system to maintain internal stability. Life changes upset stability and call for readjustment. Too much change taxes the capacity to readjust and thereby produces stress. The Family Inventory of Life Events and Changes (FILE) is a 71-item, yes-or-no response questionnaire that measures individuals' perceptions of stressful events that the family has been subjected to during the previous 12 months.

Description

Research has demonstrated a relationship between stress-producing life events and illness. A pool of 171 items was developed, using inventories that measure these and other stress-producing events identified by family stress research. Based on the frequency of responses and conceptual clarity, this pool was reduced to 75 items. Factor analysis was used (and occasionally ignored for what looked right) to produce a 17-item intrafamily strain subscale and eight other subscales measured by 54 items: marital strains (sexual and separation issues); pregnancy and childbearing strains; finance and business strains; work transition, family transition, and work strains; illness onset, chronic illness, childcare, and dependency strains; losses due to deaths and broken relationships; transitions into or out of the home; and legal violations by family members. Only the intrafamily strain subscale and the total Recent Life Changes score are recommended for use. Although weights are available for each of the 71 finally selected items varying from 19 points for the purchase of a car to 99 points for the death of a child, research shows that simply giving one point for each "yes" produces a comparable result. Sixteen items were kept despite low frequency (for example, death of child), because of the impact of such stressful events on families.

Sample

Various samples were used. Selection for the final inventory used data from 322 families who had a child chronically ill with diseases such as cerebral palsy. The factor analysis used a national survey of 2,740 primarily white Lutherans from all stages of the family life cycle. Validity checks used low- and high-conflict families with chronically ill children. Stability estimates used about 100 female and 50 male students from high school to graduate school.

Reliability

The internal consistency estimates of all the subscales except in intrafamily strain are too low (.09 to .71 with a median of .53) to advise their use even with caution. The total scale internal consistency estimates vary from .79 to .81 and estimates for the intrafamily strains subscale vary from .71 to .73. Test–retest reliability (after five weeks) is .73 for intrafamily strain and .80 for the total scale.

Validity

Total Recent Life Changes correlated significantly with pulmonary functioning of children with cystic fibrosis. In addition, there were "statistically significant correlations" (a euphemism for very slight practical use) between intrafamily strain scores or total FILE scores and paper-and-pencil self-reports of cohesion, conflict, independence of family members, and family organization. Low-conflict families reported less stress than high-conflict families.

Administration

FILE is a 71-item, yes-or-no, paper-and-pencil instrument that takes about 10 to 15 minutes of the family's and the therapist's time. Each individual answers separately. A no response is coded 1 and yes is coded 0. Percentile norms for 1,997 individuals, from young married couples to those retired, are reported.

Location

McCubbin, H. I., Patterson, J. M., & Wilson, L. R. (1985). FILE: Family Inventory of Life Events and Changes. In D. Olson, H.I. McCubbin, H. Barnes, A. Larsen, M. Muxen, & M. Wilson (Eds.), *Family inventories* (revised edition). St. Paul, MN: Family Social Science, University of Minnesota.

Discussion

The mean number of stresses reported is 8.4 for men (with 14% reporting two or fewer and 16% reporting 13 or more) and 9.2 for women (with 16% reporting three or fewer and 17% reporting 14 or more).

The authors wisely ask clinicians not to use the subscales with low reliability scores. Percentile reports must be used with caution. After all, the normal stress range for launching families (with children leaving home) is reported about 50% higher than families in the couple and preschool stage.

Stress research is usually directed the other way: How does family stress contribute to the increase of physical illness, poor academic performance, and trouble with the law? FILE measures how these woes put stress on the family. Unfortunately, the majority of validity studies with FILE have used FILE's ability to correlate with other paper-and-pencil tests. It is hardly surprising that high-conflict families score higher on the intrafamily strain subscale when that subscale specifically asks if there has been an "increase in conflict between husband and wife."

The purpose of FILE is to enable the therapist to identify those sources of stress that seriously weaken the family's flexibility. It also increases the family's own awareness of the strains they have been struggling with and encourages the family to look at all these demands and their impact on the family. The FILE concentrates on events in the past 12 months. Forms are available with events from the more distant past that still put a strain on the family.

Sample Items From FILE

1.* Increase of husband/father's time away from family.

2. Increase of wife/mother's time away from family.

3. A member appears to have emotional problems.

4. A member appears to depend on alcohol or drugs.

5. Increase in conflict between husband and wife.

6. Increase in arguments between parent(s) and child(ren).

7. Increase in conflict among children in the family.

8. Increased difficulty in managing teenage child(ren).

13. Increase in the amount of "outside activities" which the child(ren) are involved in.

14. Increased disagreement about a member's friends or activities.

15. Increase in the number of problems or issues which don't get resolved.

16. Increase in the number of tasks or chores which don't get done.

17. Increased conflict with in-laws or relatives.

18. Spouse/parent was separated or divorced.

19. Spouse/parent has an "affair."

20. Increased difficulty in resolving issues with a "former" or separated spouse.

21. Increased difficulty with sexual relationships between husband and wife.

22. Spouse had unwanted or difficult pregnancy.

23. An unmarried member became pregnant.

24. A member had an abortion.

(continued)

*Numbers indicate actual number of the item on the original FILE.

Sample Items From FILE (*continued*)

25. A member gave birth to or adopted a child.
30. A member started a new business.
32. A member purchased a car or other major item.
33. Increasing financial debts due to over-use of credit cards.
35. Increased strain on family "money" for food, clothing, energy, home care.
37. Delay in receiving child support or alimony payments.
39. A member lost or quit a job.
40. A member retired from work.
41. A member started or returned to work.
46. Family moved to a new home/apartment.
51. A member became physically disabled or chronically ill.
54. Increased responsibility to provide direct care or financial help to husband's and/or wife's parent(s).
55. Experienced difficulty in arranging for satisfactory child care.
56. A parent/spouse died.
61. A member "broke up" a relationship with a close friend.
62. A member was married.
70. A member ran away from home.
71. A member dropped out of school or was suspended from school.

*Numbers indicate actual number of the item on the original FILE.

29 | FAMILY CRISIS-ORIENTED PERSONAL EVALUATION SCALES

Hamilton I. McCubbin, David H. Olson, and Andrea S. Larsen

Introduction

McCubbin and associates have created a series of instruments to measure the stresses that affect the family (see FILE) or the adolescent's reaction to family stress (A-FILE). But it is also necessary to know what methods the family uses to cope with stress. The Family Crisis-Oriented Personal Evaluation Scales (F-COPES) is a 29-item, five-point self-report inventory that measures internal and external family strategies. The internal strategies are the ways family members deal with crisis by using resources within the family, such as confidence in problem solving, ability to face change, and passive, inactive behaviors. External strategies include active behavior the family uses to acquire resources outside the family system, such as religious resource, relatives and grandparents, friends, neighbors, and community resources.

Description

A review of the literature identified 49 methods families use in coping with crises. Factor analysis reduced this list to 30. One other item, "exercising to stay fit" (number 18), was also deleted from the final scale. The list can be conceptualized as comprising five subscales (number of items in parentheses):

- Acquiring social support (9): ability to try to get help from relatives, friends, neighbors, and grandparents;
- Reframing (8): ability to redefine crises to make them more manageable;
- Seeking spiritual support (4);
- Mobilizing family to acquire and accept help (4); and
- Passive appraisal (4): ability to ignore problem and minimize reaction.

Individuals taking F-COPES respond to each item by checking "strongly agree," "agree," "neither agree nor disagree," "disagree," or "strongly disagree."

Sample

The factor analysis that produced F-COPES used students in one course at the University of Minnesota, their families, and their friends. A large percentage were working professionals in the area of human services. Final reliability studies used 2,582 white Lutherans from a national sample.

Reliability

Internal consistency reliability estimates for the final instrument were: acquiring social support, .83; reframing, .82; seeking spiritual support, .80; mobilizing family to acquire and accept help, .71; passive appraisal, .63; and total scale, .86.

Stability estimate of the F-COPES scores after four weeks was .61 for reframing, .75 to .95 for other subscales, and .81 for the total inventory.

Validity

Although factor analysis did demonstrate the existence of five independent concepts, no other validity data are reported other than the surface appeal of the items.

Administration

F-COPES takes about 10 minutes to complete. The words and phrases are simple enough for preadolescents, except perhaps for the phrase, "Facing the problems 'head-on.'" Percentile norms are available for the five subscales.

Location

McCubbin, H., Larsen, A., & Olson, D. (1985). F-COPES: Family Crisis Oriented Personal Evaluation Scales. In D. Olson, H. McCubbin, H. Barnes, A. Larsen, M. Muxen, & M. Wilson (Eds.), *Family inventories* (revised edition). St. Paul, MN: Family Social Science, University of Minnesota.

Discussion

This is another measurement tool for the clinician and researcher still new enough that copies are printed with an item that has been eliminated from the final instrument.

The total scale, although of moderate reliability, contains items that seem, at least conceptually, to belong to different worlds. "Believing if we wait long enough, the problem will go away" and "Seeking professional counseling" are both coping techniques. What does it mean when two such different items are added together to produce a total score? It would be nice, although difficult, for research to discover which technique is more effective in promoting marital happiness.

The subscales show greater promise for therapy and research than the total scale. Using subscales, the therapist and clients can see which coping method is being used. At present, F-COPES is not printed in a form to facilitate subscale use.

F-COPES
Family Crisis-Oriented Personal Scales

PURPOSE

The Family Crisis Oriented Personal Evaluation Scales is designed to record effective problem-solving attitudes and behavior which families develop to respond to problems or difficulties.

WHEN WE FACE PROBLEMS OR DIFFICULTIES IN OUR FAMILY, WE RESPOND BY:

1	Sharing our difficulties with relatives
2	Seeking encouragement and support from friends
3	Knowing we have the power to solve major problems
4	Seeking information and advice from persons in other families who have faced the same or similar problems
5	Seeking advice from relatives (grandparents, etc.)
6	Seeking assistance from community agencies and programs designed to help families in our situation
7	Knowing that we have the strength within our own family to solve our problems
8	Receiving gifts and favors from neighbors (e.g. food, taking in mail, etc.)
9	Seeking information and advice from the family doctor
10	Asking neighbors for favors and assistance

(continued)

WHEN WE FACE PROBLEMS OR DIFFICULTIES IN OUR FAMILY, WE RESPOND BY:

11	Facing the problems "head-on" and trying to get solution right away
12	Watching television
13	Showing that we are strong
14	Attending church services
15	Accepting stressful events as a fact of life
16	Sharing concerns with close friends
17	Knowing luck plays a big part in how well we are able to solve family problems
18*	Exercising with friends to stay fit and reduce tension
19	Accepting that difficulties occur unexpectedly
20	Doing things with relatives (get-togethers, dinners, etc.)
21	Seeking professional counseling and help for family difficulties
22	Believing we can handle our own problems
23	Participating in church activities
24	Defining the family problem in a more positive way so that we do not become too discouraged
25	Asking relatives how they feel about problems we face
26	Feeling that no matter what we do to prepare, we will have difficulty handling problems
27	Seeking advice from a minister
28	Believing if we wait long enough, the problem will go away
29	Sharing problems with neighbors
30	Having faith in God

*Deleted from final scale.

30 | PREPARE-ENRICH INVENTORIES

David G. Fournier, David H. Olson, and Joan M. Druckman

Introduction

The PREPARE-ENRICH Inventories are part of a comprehensive package of materials and procedures designed to meet the needs of professionals engaged in marriage preparation, marriage enrichment, and marriage therapy. The inventory titles not only briefly describe the inventories, but they are also clever—perhaps too clever—acronyms: PREPARE stands for PREmarital Personal And Relationship Evaluation; PREPARE-MC stands for PREmarital Personal And Relationship Evaluation—Marriage with Children; and ENRICH stands for Evaluating and Nurturing Relationship Issues, Communication, and Happiness. In addition to the item booklets for PREPARE, PREPARE-MC, and ENRICH, numerous other printed and computer-generated documents have been developed to facilitate use of the inventories.

PREPARE and PREPARE-MC serve as preventive tools so that couples will be more aware of important relationship issues before problems become too serious. ENRICH is designed for couples seeking marriage therapy and marriage enrichment.

Description

In the fall of 1976, Olson and colleagues began a series of evaluation studies of marriage preparation programs. Other instruments proved inappropriate so PREPARE was developed from three previous instruments the Olson team had used. PREPARE's success as a research device led to its modification for clinical use in 1979. In 1981 two modified forms were added: PREPARE-MC for engaged couples who have at least one child from a previous relationship, and ENRICH for married couples seeking therapy.

The three inventories contain the following categories (with the number of items in parenthesis):

- Idealistic Distortion (15 PREPARE, 5 ENRICH)
- Realistic Expectations (10 PREPARE)
- Marital Satisfaction (10 ENRICH)

For both PREPARE and ENRICH:

- Personality Issues (10)
- Communication (10)
- Conflict Resolution (10)
- Financial Management (10)
- Leisure Activities (10)
- Sexual Relationship (10)
- Children and Marriage (10)
- Family and Friends (10)
- Equalitarian Roles (10)
- Religious Orientation (10)

Sample

Nationwide samples of 5,718 individuals for PREPARE and 1,344 individuals for ENRICH were used. The PREPARE sample represents a good cross-section of engaged individuals. The ENRICH sample was derived from probability sampling.

PREPARE-ENRICH raw scores are converted into percentile scores so that each individual can be compared relative to national norms. Individual percentile scores were calculated for both male and female partners for each of the 12 content categories in PREPARE and 14 categories in ENRICH.

Reliability

PREPARE internal consistency reliabilities range from a low of .49 for Children and Marriage to a high of .88 for Idealistic Distortion. The median internal consistency reliability is .70. Test-retest reliabilities (testing was separated by four weeks) ranged from .64 for Sexual Relationship to .93 for Religious Orientation, with a median test-retest reliability of .79.

ENRICH internal consistency reliabilities vary from .48 for Sexual Relationship to .92 for Idealistic Distortion with a median internal consistency reliability of .76. ENRICH test-retest reliabilities (testing was separated by four weeks) varied from .77 for Leisure Activities to .92 for both Sexual Relationship and Idealistic Distortion. The median test-retest reliability was a high .89. These are sufficient for research purposes and the tests can be used with caution to determine differences that exist between individuals and sample norms. The internal consistency reliabilities are not high enough for predictive testing.

Validity

The content of the PREPARE-ENRICH Inventories was specifically developed to identify the most frequently found conflicts in marital studies. All 12 scales were significantly correlated with the Locke-Wallace Marital Adjustment Scale. Significant relationships were established between PREPARE-ENRICH scales and existing measures of relationship conflict, esteem, communication, empathy, egalitarianism, assertiveness, temperament, cohesion, and independence.

Factor analysis revealed 11 unique factors. The categories, Personality Issues and Communication, merged to account for one rather than the expected two factors. Most categories contained only one significant factor verifying a predominantly unidimensional structure for each scale.

A three-year follow-up study of 164 couples who took PREPARE during their engagement was able to predict with 80% to 90% accuracy which couples separated and divorced and which were happily married (Flowers & Olson, 1986).

Administration

The PREPARE-ENRICH Inventories are eight-page booklets that contain 125 items pertaining to marital issues. The items relate to the individual, the partner, and the relationship rather than to marriage in general. All items (excluding the final 10 on ENRICH) are answered on a five-point, Likert-type scale, from 1 point for "strongly agree" to 5 points for "strongly disagree."

PREPARE-ENRICH answer sheets are specially printed documents designed to be optically scanned for computer processing. The front page of each answer sheet contains 19 demographic and contextual questions and a special identification section using number codes for the couple and for the therapist. The sheets are color-coded to prevent confusion.

PREPARE-ENRICH scoring includes a 15-20-page computer printout specially designed to highlight individual and couple scores, national norm scores, and clearly labeled listings of each person's responses to all inventory items. Each computer printout includes a set of couple feedback forms designed to facilitate the process of discussing results with the couple. Also returned with each computer-processed inventory is a specially printed therapist feedback form. This form is designed to help the therapist organize results and to make choices about issues most in need of discussion.

Location

Olson, D. H., Fournier, D. G., & Druckman, J. M. (1982). *PREPARE-ENRICH: Counselor's manual*. Minneapolis: Prepare-Enrich Inc.

Discussion

PREPARE-ENRICH is the most professional-looking marriage-therapy-testing package available. The *Counselor's Manual* is thorough, well printed, and helpful. The printouts focus on "relationship strengths" and what are euphemistically called "work areas," rather than relationship weaknesses. The instruments are designed as an aid to initial assessment. Couples usually find the procedures to be meaningful to their relationship and therapists enjoy the flexibility and comprehensiveness of the information provided. A tape is available providing model sessions using the package, and a one-day workshop is advised so that overenthusiastic therapists will not use the package beyond its limitations ("to predict couple happiness or to block an impending marriage"). Therapists who use computer printouts become aware of the inappropriate awe with which clients sometimes regard them.

There is no self-scoring component available and the two-week wait for computer printouts must be planned. Most of the internal consistency reliabilities are much too low, especially the Sexual Relationship subscale. The warnings never to use the instruments for selection purposes cannot be repeated often enough. It is a paradox that the most attractive-looking and one of the most popular marriage instruments should lack the reliability of other less popular instruments by the same author(s). Perhaps its use as a technique overshadows its weaknesses as a measurement tool.

REFERENCE

Flowers, B., & Olson, D. (1986). Predicting marital success with PREPARE: A predictive validity study. *Journal of Marital and Family Therapy, 12(4)*, 403–413.

Sample Items from PREPARE-ENRICH

Personality Issues
Sometimes I have difficulty dealing with my partner's moodiness.
Communication
My partner should know what I'm feeling without being told.
Conflict Resolution
In order to end an argument, I usually give up and agree.
Financial Management
Sometimes I wish my partner was more careful in spending money.
Leisure Activities
I sometimes feel pressured to participate in activities that my partner enjoys.
Sexual Relationship
Sometimes I am concerned because my partner wants me to do things sexual that I do not enjoy.
Children and Marriage
I have some concerns about how my partner will be as a parent or stepparent.
Family and Friends
I am worried that one of our families may cause trouble in our marriage.
Equalitarian Roles
In our marriage, the wife should have almost all of the responsibilities for child-rearing.
Religious Orientation
My partner and I disagree about some of the teachings of our religion.

31 | PERSONAL ASSESSMENT OF INTIMACY IN RELATIONSHIPS

David H. Olson and Mark T. Schaefer

Introduction

Most men and women find energy to live autonomous, self-generating, and satisfying lives through mutually existing in the thoughts, behaviors, and affections of another. The Personal Assessment of Intimacy in Relationships (PAIR) Inventory is a 36-item questionnaire that describes how each of the partners sees the relationship as it is now and how each would like it to be on five types of intimacy: emotional, social, sexual, intellectual, and recreational.

Description

Olson (1977) identified seven kinds of intimacy:

- Emotional: sharing feelings;
- Social: sharing friends;
- Intellectual: sharing ideas;
- Sexual: sharing sex life;
- Recreational: sharing pastimes;
- Spiritual: sharing faith and values; and
- Aesthetic: sharing beauty.

Statements were solicited from family professionals, lay groups, and graduates about intimacy in general and the seven kinds of intimacy in particular. These statements were transformed into 350 potential items. Of these, 113 were selected that were conceptually related, clear, and appropriate to the categories. After a pilot study, 10 items were selected for each of the scales according to their ability to meet the following criteria: 1) not everyone or almost everyone should answer the item the same way; 2) the item should correlate higher with its own scale than with other scales; 3) factor analysis should discover the best items in each scale; and 4) an equal number of items can be found that are positively and negatively scored for each scale. Another sample was tested.

Two scales did not produce a sufficient number of reliable items: aesthetic intimacy and spiritual intimacy. The final PAIR has six items for each of five scales, plus another six items that reveal the tendency to try to make an exaggerated good impression from Edmond's Conventionality Scale (1967). Six scores are reported; a single "total" score, even without the Conventionality Scale, would be meaningless.

Sample

The pilot study used 60 women and 25 men aged 18 to 61 (median age, 29), more than half of whom were married. They were all students or from a community enrichment group. The final inventory was normed on a group of 192 nonclinical couples before they began an enrichment weekend. Follow-up studies were conducted.

Reliability

The internal consistency reliability of the PAIR is barely acceptable: from .70 for intellectual or recreational intimacy to .77 for sexual intimacy. This is about as good as can be expected from a six-item scale. No text-retest reliability is reported.

Validity

The correlation between PAIR scores and other test scores was significant and on one occasion spectacular. The Social Intimacy subscale correlated .98 with couple scores on the Locke-Wallace Marital Adjustment Scale. The correlation between PAIR and a test of self-disclosure was significant, but quite low (.13 to .31). PAIR was correlated significantly with various measures of family environment, especially Cohesion and Expressiveness. The best scale for predicting other marital questionnaire scores is the scale for Emotional Intimacy.

Administration

PAIR is a paper-and-pencil inventory in which each partner indicates on a five-point scale his or her degree of agreement with each of 36 items. The instrument can be hand-scored quickly and inexpensively. The partners describe the marriage twice: as the marriage is now and as they would like it to be. The "perceived" and "expected" scores for each partner can be plotted on a profile percentile chart to facilitate feedback. The conventionality score reveals the good impression the partners are trying to make.

Location

Olson, D. H., & Schaefer, M. T. (undated). PAIR: Personal Assessment of Intimacy in Relationships, procedure manual. St. Paul, MN: Family Social Science, University of Minnesota.

Discussion

The PAIR is a short, inexpensive questionnaire of considerable face validity and some empirical validity. Its short length means that reliability is sacrificed for convenience. Test scores must be interpreted with caution. It would prove interesting to measure the PAIR on its ability to predict eye contact, physical proximity, discussion topic, and amount of smiling, as well as paper-and-pencil scores.

Why is the sixth scale, the Conventionality score, not plotted when the marriage is described as the partners would like it to be? Is it assumed that everyone would like the marriage to be perfect? If so, then "would like it to be" should not be translated as "expected," the way the profile names these responses.

The PAIR can be used with marriage enrichment groups. It takes the concept of intimacy out of the nebulous, magical, ill-defined world of romance and becomes itself a help in providing insight into the couple's own unrealized perceptions and expectations. It shares knowledge about what each partner feels he or she is sharing and wants to share.

The fact that the authors were unable to measure aesthetic and spiritual intimacy means that these dimensions, when examined by the therapist, need to be interpreted with even more caution than those dimensions that can be measured.

Of course, there is a danger that any instrument can be converted into a weapon, especially if the unskilled therapist overemphasizes numbers.

REFERENCES

Edwards, V. (1967). Marital conventionalization: Definition and measurements. *Journal of Marriage and the Family, 29*, 681–688.

Olson, D. (1977). Communication and intimacy. Unpublished manuscript, University of Nebraska.

Personal Assessment of Intimacy in Relationships

I. EMOTIONAL INTIMACY

*1. My partner listens to me when I need someone to talk to.
7. I can state my feelings without him/her getting defensive.
13. I often feel distant from my partner.
19. My partner can really understand my hurts and joys.
25. I feel neglected at times by my partner.
31. I sometimes feel lonely when we're together.

II. SOCIAL INTIMACY

2. We enjoy spending time with other couples.
8. We usually "keep to ourselves."
14. We have very few friends in common.
20. Having time together with friends is an important part of our shared activities.
26. Many of my partner's closest friends are also my closest friends.
32. My partner disapproves of some of my friends.

III. SEXUAL INTIMACY

3. I am satisfied with our sex life.
9. I feel our sexual activity is just routine.
15. I am able to tell my partner when I want sexual intercourse.
21. I "hold back" my sexual interest because my partner makes me feel uncomfortable.
27. Sexual expression is an essential part of our relationship.
33. My partner seems disinterested in sex.

IV. INTELLECTUAL INTIMACY

4. My partner helps me clarify my thoughts.
10. When it comes to having a serious discussion it seems that we have little in common.
16. I feel "put down" in a serious conversation with my partner.
22. I feel it is useless to discuss some things with my partner.
28. My partner frequently tries to change my ideas.
34. We have an endless number of things to talk about.

V. RECREATIONAL INTIMACY

5. We enjoy the same recreational activities.
11. I share in very few of my partner's interests.
17. We like playing together.
23. We enjoy the out-of-doors together.
29. We seldom find time to do fun things together.
35. I think that we share some of the same interests.

VI. CONVENTIONALITY SCALE

6. My partner has all the qualities I've ever wanted in a mate.
12. There are times when I do not feel a great deal of love and affection for my partner.
18. Every new thing that I have learned about my partner has pleased me.
24. My partner and I understand each other completely.
30. I don't think anyone could possibly be happier than my partner and I when we are with one another.
36. I have some needs that are not being met by my relationship.

*Numbers indicate order of item in commercially sold inventory.

8
Epilogue

One of the main distinctions between a profession and a job is an organized body of research available for and required by the practitioner. This research usually demands reliable and valid instrumentation. But instruments are more than research evaluators to the family therapist. They are valuable ways of provoking insights into feelings and stimulating behavior changes.

This handbook describes instruments developed or revised since 1975. We have found marriage and family instrumentation moving in particular directions.

Directions

1. There is a powerful thrust towards *higher* standards and greater rigor in research and practice. This is promoted by professional associations, journal editors, the increasing number of family therapy doctoral programs in the universities, and state licensing laws.
2. Family research centers and universities stimulate an obligation to

publish. There is an explosion of new books and journals in the field.

3. The computer has made more sophisticated statistical and research designs possible for the development of instruments and the processing and analysis of data.
4. More instruments are being invented to deal with or assess very specific problems rather than general issues.
5. Several professional journals have begun to pay more attention to measurement instruments and outcome research. For example, *The American Journal of Family Therapy* introduced a section to describe and review tests.
6. Church-affiliated centers have taken strong steps in premarital therapy. They have the advantage that they can require some form of counseling as a prerequisite to a desired church ceremony. Such counseling or therapy can focus on normality and development rather than crisis and pathology. Many instruments in this handbook were developed with a Lutheran population. Considerable promise is shown by material developed in the Catholic Church's premarital (Pre-Cana) and marital enrichment (Cana) Conferences.
7. Videotape systems enable clients, especially adolescents, to see themselves as others see them. They also enable evaluators to measure interactions. Videotape analysis, for all its time consumption, is on the frontier of research.

What Is Needed

1. Studies are needed that demonstrate the *predictive validity* of marital instruments rather than the not very helpful ability to distinguish between two presently existing groups of satisfied and dissatisfied couples.
2. There is a need to develop instruments that are not paper-and-pencil type but are based on standardized, structured interview techniques.

3. There remains the need to measure the family system. The family is a system. Testing is a measure of individual differences. Marriage and family testing at one level thus remains a paradox or, at least, a constant challenge.
4. A breakthrough remains to be made before the videotape analysis inventory can be used by clinicians and marriage therapy educators. Unfortunately, interaction analysis requires an immense amount of training and time.
5. Some special instrumentation needs to be developed for specific use by the expert witness in divorce and custody procedures.
6. Greater recognition is needed of the influence of culture on behavior, values, satisfaction, and expected role.
7. There is some recognition of client reaction to the therapist. Instruments remain to be developed that would measure the effect of the therapist on the kind of therapeutic system evolved and upon the outcomes of the therapy.
8. Norm samples are needed that are not uniquely members of a specific religious, racial, social, or educational group.
9. Most popular family therapy theories, such as structural, strategic, and systemic approaches, find little use for tests and inventories in clinical practice. Test constructors need to demonstrate that the data obtainable by administration of such instruments are sufficiently different from or more accurate than or more time efficient than what is obtainable in the interview by a typically trained practitioner.
10. The results of marriage and family testing do not yet yield the kind of numbers that have the weight of I.Q. scores for making predictions or the quality of analysis extracted from the Rorschach to explain behavior.

So what has been accomplished? In this handbook, we have described 35 observational techniques and self-report instruments and commented on how 11 nonfamily inventories are being used with families. These measurements can be used by researchers and therapists to gain insight into the family process and to help in improving family relationships both developmentally and remedially. Some of these instruments are already being revised. Year by year we see improvements in both the quality and the extent of coverage in terms of what is being measured. Whether artistically applied as clinical techniques or utilized as objective measures, these instruments do help to evaluate and promote the therapeutic process.